The Wisdom of James Allen III

- Out from the Heart
- Byways of Blessedness
- From Passion to Peace
- The Heavenly Life

The Wisdom of James Allen III

Four Classic Works from the author of *As a Man Thinketh*

- Out from the Heart
- Byways of Blessedness
- From Passion to Peace
- The Heavenly Life

Laurel Creek Press
San Diego, California 2004

Laurel Creek Press is a project of the Blue Dove Foundation, an independent, nonprofit organization dedicated to making available the finest spiritual works from the world's religions and wisdom traditions. For a free catalog contact:

The Blue Dove Foundation
P.O. Box 261611
San Diego, CA 92196
858-623-3330 or 800-691-1008
www.laurelcreekpress.com or www.bluedove.org

Copyright © 2004 Laurel Creek Press, All Rights Reserved
8 7 6 5 4 3 2 1

The Wisdom of James Allen III
Edited by Andy Zubko. This book contains the complete and unabridged text of each of the four listed works. For clarity, some obscure or archaic English words and phrases were rendered into modern usage. James Allen used the generic masculine in his writings, as was the common practice of his time. This was retained in order to remain true to his voice.

Cover and Text Design: Brian Moucka. Special thanks to Kimberly Davis, Russell Morioka, and Melanie Smith for their dedicated efforts in the production of this book.

Library of Congress Cataloging-in-Publication Data
```
Allen, James, 1864-1912
    The wisdom of James Allen III : Laurel Creek
James Allen wisdom series / James Allen
       p. cm.
ISBN 1-889606-08-1 (perfect bound)
1. New Thought. I. Title
BF639 .A672 2000
289.9'8--dc21
                        00-061207 CIP
```

About James Allen

JAMES ALLEN has been called the "literary mystery man" of the twentieth century. Although his best-selling classic, *As a Man Thinketh*, has inspired millions around the world, little is known about the author himself.

What is known about James Allen is that he was born in 1864 in Leicester, England. His father was a well-to-do businessman who, because of poor economic conditions, went bankrupt in 1878 and was tragically murdered one year later. This required James to leave school at the age of fifteen to help support his family. James eventually married and became a personal secretary for an executive of a large English corporation.

At the age of 38, James Allen reached what can be called a crossroads in his life. Influenced by the writings of Tolstoy, James came to the realization that a life devoted to making money and spending it on frivolous activities was a meaningless way to live.

He retired from his employment and moved with his wife to a small cottage on the southwest shore of England to pursue a life of contemplation. It was here at Iltracombe that James pursued his dream of voluntary poverty, spiritual self-discipline, and a life of simplicity as taught by his mentor, Tolstoy.

A typical James Allen day would be to rise very early in the morning and walk to a bluff overlooking the ocean, where he would remain in meditation for an hour or so. And as the cobwebs which had obscured his spiritual vision lifted, the secrets of the universe would unfold before him. Quietly these impressions would be recorded within. Afterwards, he would return home and pen his insights on paper. Afternoons were committed to tending his garden; evenings to communion with townsfolk who wished to discuss loftier philosophical issues.

For ten years James Allen led this quiet, pensive life, earning a small stipend from royalties paid on his writing. Then suddenly, at the age of 48, he passed away. He died the way he lived, a virtual unknown, untouched by fame, unrewarded by fortune. It would only be after his death that the reading public would come to recognize the genius and inspiration of his work. But this is the way the anonymous English

~ About James Allen

mystic would have wanted it—to posthumously share his spiritual insights with the world.

James Allen's classic work, *As a Man Thinketh*, as well as *The Path to Prosperity*, *The Way of Peace*, *The Mastery of Destiny*, and *Entering the Kingdom* have all been combined in the first volume of this set, *The Wisdom of James Allen*.

Book Two, *The Wisdom of James Allen II*, includes three more James Allen titles: *Light on Life's Difficulties*, *Above Life's Turmoil*, and *The Life Triumphant*.

This third book, *The Wisdom of James Allen III*, contains these four timeless works: *Out from the Heart*, *Byways of Blessedness*, *From Passion to Peace*, and *The Heavenly Life*. These books are his loving bequest to the world.

Foreword

I LOOKED AROUND UPON THE WORLD, and saw that it was shadowed by sorrow and scorched by the fierce fires of suffering. And I looked for the cause. I looked around, but I could not find it; I looked in books, but I could not find it; I looked within, and found there both the cause and the self-made nature of that cause. I looked again, and deeper, and found the remedy. I found one Law, the Law of Love; one Life, the life of adjustment to that Law; one Truth, the Truth of a conquered mind and a quiet and obedient heart.

And I dreamed of writing books which would help men and women, whether rich or poor, learned or unlearned, worldly or unworldly to find within themselves the source of all success, all happiness, all accomplishment, all truth. And the dream remained with me, and at last became substantial; and now I send forth these books into the world on a mission of healing and blessedness, knowing that they cannot fail to reach the homes and hearts of those who are waiting and ready to receive them.

—*James Allen*

Contents:

Book One: Out From The Heart..................15

Book Two: Byways of Blessedness................63

Book Three: From Passion to Peace.............249

Book Four: The Heavenly Life.....................295

The Wisdom of James Allen III

- Out from the Heart
- Byways of Blessedness
- From Passion to Peace
- The Heavenly Life

Make pure thy heart,
    and thou wilt make thy life
Rich, sweet, and beautiful, unmarred by strife;
Guard well thy mind,
    and, noble, strong, and free,
Nothing shall harm, disturb, or conquer thee;
For all thy foes are in thy heart and mind,
There also thy salvation thou wilt find.

BOOK ONE

ut from the Heart

OUT FROM THE HEART

TABLE OF CONTENTS

The Heart and The Life..17

The Nature and Power of Mind............................20

Formation of Habit..24

Doing and Knowing...29

First Steps in The Higher Life..............................34

Mental Conditions and Their Effects...................53

Exhortation...59

The Heart and The Life

AS THE HEART, SO IS THE LIFE. The within is ceaselessly becoming the without. Nothing remains unrevealed. That which is hidden is but for a time; it ripens and comes forth at last. Seed, tree, blossom, and fruit are the fourfold order of the universe. From the state of a man's heart proceed the conditions of his life. His thoughts blossom into deeds; and his deeds bear the fruitage of character and destiny.

Life is ever unfolding from within, and revealing itself to the light, and thoughts engendered in the heart at last reveal themselves in words, actions, and things accomplished.

As the fountain from the hidden spring, so flows

forth a man's life from the secret recesses of his heart. All that he is and does is generated there. All that he will be and do will take its rise there.

Sorrow and happiness, suffering and enjoyment, fear and hope, hatred and love, ignorance and enlightenment, are nowhere but in the heart. They are solely mental conditions.

The Witness of The Mind

Man is the keeper of his heart; the watcher of his mind; the solitary guard of his citadel of life. As such, he can be diligent or negligent. He can keep his heart more and more carefully. He can more strenuously watch and purify his mind; and he can guard against the thinking of unrighteous thoughts—this is the way of enlightenment and bliss.

On the other hand, he can live loosely and carelessly, neglecting the supreme task of rightfully ordering his life—this is the way of self-delusion and suffering.

Let a man realize that life in its totality proceeds from the mind, and lo, the way of blessedness is opened up to him! For he will then discover that he possesses the power to rule his mind, and to fashion it in accordance with his Ideal. So will he elect to strongly and steadfastly walk those pathways of thought and action which are altogether excellent. To him, life will become beautiful and sacred; and sooner or later, he will put to flight all evil, confusion, and suffering. For it is impossible for a man to fall short of liberation, enlightenment, and peace, who guards with unwearying diligence the gateway of his heart.

The Nature and Power of Mind

MIND IS THE ARBITER of life. It is the creator and shaper of conditions, and the recipient of its own results. It contains within itself both the power to create illusion and to perceive reality.

Mind is the infallible weaver of destiny. Thought is the thread, good and evil deeds are the "warp and woof" or foundation, and the web, woven upon the loom of life, is character. Mind clothes itself in garments of its own making.

Man, as a mental being, possesses all the powers of mind, and is furnished with unlimited choice. He learns by experience, and he can accelerate or retard his experience. He is not arbitrarily bound at any point, but he has bound himself at many points, and having bound himself he can, when he chooses, liberate himself.

He can become bestial or pure, ignorant or noble, foolish or wise, just as he chooses. He can, by reoccurring practice, form habits, and he can, by renewed effort, break them off. He can surround himself with illusions until Truth is completely lost, and he can destroy each of those illusions until Truth is entirely recovered. His possibilities are endless; his freedom is complete.

The Outer Is Molded by The Inner

It is the nature of the mind to create its own conditions, and to choose the states in which it shall dwell. It also has the power to alter any condition, to abandon any state. This it is continually doing as it gathers knowledge of state after state by repeated choice and exhaustive experience.

Inward processes of thought make up the sum of character and life. Man can modify and alter these processes by bringing will and effort to bear upon them. The bonds of habit, impotence, and sin are self-made, and can only be destroyed by one's self. They exist nowhere but in one's mind, and although they are directly related to outward things, they have no real existence in those things.

The outer is molded and animated by the inner, and never the inner by the outer. Temptation does not arise in the outer object, but in the lust of the mind for that object. Nor do sorrow and suffering belong by nature to the external things and happenings of life, but in an undisciplined attitude of mind toward those things and happenings.

The mind that is disciplined by Purity and fortified by Wisdom avoids all those lusts and desires which are inseparately bound up with affliction, and so arrives at enlightenment and peace.

Transforming Your Life

To condemn others as evil, and to curse at outside conditions as the source of evil, increases and does not lessen, the world's suffering and unrest. The outer is but the shadow and effect of the inner, and when the heart is pure all outward things are pure.

All growth and life is from within outward; all decay and death is from without inward. This is the universal law. All evolution proceeds from within. All adjustment must take place within. He who ceases to strive against others, and employs his powers in the transformation, regeneration, and development of his own mind, conserves his energies and preserves himself. And as he succeeds in harmonizing his own mind, he leads others by consideration and charity into a like blessed state.

~ Out from the Heart

The way of enlightenment and peace is not gained by assuming authority and guidance over other minds, but by exercising a lawful authority over one's own mind, and by guiding one's self in pathways of steadfast and lofty virtue.

A man's life proceeds from his heart and his mind. He has compounded that mind by his own thoughts and deeds. It is within his power to refashion that mind by his choice of thought. In this manner he can transform his life. Let us see how this is to be done.

Formation of Habit

EVERY ESTABLISHED mental condition is an acquired habit, and it has become such by continuous repetition of thought. Despondency and cheerfulness, anger and calmness, covetousness and generosity—indeed, all states of mind—are habits built up by choice, until they have become automatic. A thought constantly repeated at last becomes a fixed habit of the mind, and from such habits proceeds one's life.

It is in the nature of the mind to acquire knowledge by the repetition of its experiences. A thought which is very difficult, at first, to hold and dwell upon, at last becomes, by constantly being held in the mind, a natural and habitual practice.

A boy, when commencing to learn a trade, cannot even handle his tools right, much less use them cor-

~ Out from the Heart

rectly, but after long repetition and practice, he plies them with perfect ease and consummate skill. Likewise, a state of mind, at first apparently incapable of realization, is, by perseverance and practice, at last acquired and built into the character as a natural and spontaneous condition.

In this power of the mind to form and reform its habits, its conditions, is contained the basis of a man's salvation. It is the open door to perfect liberty by the mastery of self. For as a man has the power to form harmful habits, so he equally has the same power to create habits that are essentially good. And here we come to a point which needs some clarifying, and which calls for deep and earnest thought on the part of my reader.

It Is Easier to Do Wrong Than Right

It is commonly said to be easier to do wrong than right, to sin than to be holy. Such a condition has come to be regarded, almost universally, as a self-evident truth.

No less a teacher than the Buddha has said: "Bad deeds, and deeds hurtful to ourselves, are easy to do; what is beneficial and good, that is very difficult to do."

And with regards to humanity generally, this is true, but it is only true as a passing experience, a fleeting factor in human evolution. It is not a fixed condition of things. It is not the nature of an eternal truth. It is easier for men to do wrong than right, because of the prevalence of ignorance, because the true nature of things, and the essence and meaning of life, are not understood.

To Think Rightly Requires Practice

When a child is learning to write, it is extremely easy to hold the pen wrongly, and to form his letters incorrectly, but it is painfully difficult to hold the pen and to write properly. This is because of the child's ignorance of the art of writing, which can only be dispelled by persistent effort and practice, until, at last, it becomes natural and easy to hold the pen correctly, and difficult, as well as altogether unnecessary, to do the wrong thing.

It is the same in the vital things of mind and life. To think and do rightly requires much practice and renewed effort. But the time comes at last when it becomes habitual and easy to think and do rightly, and difficult, as it is then seen to be altogether unnecessary, to do that which is wrong.

Just as an artisan becomes, by practice, accomplished in his craft, so you can become, by prac-

~ Out from the Heart

tice, accomplished in goodness. It is entirely a matter of forming new habits of thought. And he to whom right thoughts have become easy and natural, and wrong thoughts and acts difficult to do, has attained to the highest virtue, to pure spiritual knowledge.

Sin and Virtue Are Both Formed by Habit

It is easy and natural for men to sin because they have formed by incessant repetition, harmful and unenlightened habits of thought. It is very difficult for the thief to refrain from stealing when the opportunity occurs, because he has lived so long in covetous and greedy thoughts.

But such difficulty does not exist for the honest man who has lived so long with upright and honest thoughts. He has thereby become so enlightened as to the wrong, folly, and fruitlessness of theft, that even the remotest idea of stealing does not enter his mind. The sin of theft is a very extreme one, and I have introduced it in order to more clearly illustrate the force and formation of habit. But all sins and virtues are formed in the same way.

Anger and impatience are natural and easy to thousands of people, because they are constantly repeating angry and impatient thoughts and acts. And with each repetition the habit is more firmly established and more deeply rooted.

Calmness and patience can become habitual in the same way—by first grasping through effort, a calm and patient thought, and then continuously thinking it, and living in it, until "use becomes second nature," and anger and impatience pass away forever. It is in this manner that every wrong thought may be expelled from the mind; that every untrue act may be destroyed; that every sin may be overcome.

Doing and Knowing

LET A MAN REALIZE that his life, in its totality, proceeds from his mind. Let him realize that the mind is a combination of habits which he can, by patient effort, modify to any extent, and over which he can thus gain complete ascendancy, mastery, and control. At once, he will have obtained possession of the key which shall open the door to his complete emancipation.

But freedom from the ills of life (which are the ills of one's mind) is a matter of steady growth from within, and not a sudden acquisition from without. Hourly and daily must the mind be trained to think stainless thoughts, and adapt right and dispassionate attitudes under those circumstances in which it is prone to fall into wrong and passion. Like the patient sculptor upon his marble, the aspirant to the Right

Life must gradually work upon the crude material of his mind until he has wrought out of it the Ideal of his holiest dreams.

Step by Step Progression

In working toward such supreme accomplishment, it is necessary to begin at the lowest and easiest steps, and proceed by natural, progressive stages to the higher and more difficult. This law of growth, progress, evolution, and unfoldment, by gradual and ever ascending stages, is absolute in every department of life, and in every human accomplishment. Where it is ignored, total failure will result.

In acquiring education, in learning a trade, or in pursuing a business, this law is fully recognized and minutely obeyed by all. But in acquiring Virtue, in learning Truth, and in pursuing the right conduct and knowledge of life, it is unrecognized and disobeyed by nearly all. Hence Virtue, Truth, and the Perfect Life remain unpracticed, unacquired, and unknown.

Practice Always Precedes Knowledge

It is a common error to suppose that the Higher Life is a matter of reading, and the adoption of theological or metaphysical hypotheses, and that Spiritual

~ Out from the Heart

Principles can be understood by this method. The Higher Life is higher living in thought, word, and deed, and the knowledge of those Spiritual Principles which are imminent in man and in the universe can only be acquired after long discipline in the pursuit and practice of Virtue.

The lesser must be thoroughly grasped and understood before the greater can be known. Practice always precedes real knowledge.

The schoolmaster never attempts to teach his pupils the abstract principles of mathematics at the start. He knows that such a method of teaching would be in vain, and learning impossible. He first places before them a simple sum, and, having explained it, leaves them to do it. When, after repeated failures and ever renewed effort, they have succeeded in doing it correctly, a more difficult task is set before them, and then another and another. It is not until the pupils have, through many years of diligent application, mastered all the lessons in arithmetic, that he attempts to unfold to them the underlying mathematical principles.

In learning a trade, say that of a mechanic, a boy is not at first taught the principles of mechanics, but a simple tool is put in his hand and he is told how rightly to use it. He is then left to do it by effort and practice. As he succeeds in plying his tools correctly, more and more difficult tasks are set before him, until after several years of successful practice, he is prepared to study and grasp the principles of mechanics.

In a properly governed household, the child is first taught to be obedient, and to conduct himself properly under all circumstances. The child is not even told why he must do this, but is commanded to do it. Only after he has far succeeded in doing what is right and proper, is he told why he should do it. No father would attempt to teach his child the principles of ethics before exacting from him the practice of family duty and social virtue.

Thus practice ever precedes knowledge even in the ordinary things of the world, and in spiritual things, in the living of the Higher Life, this law is rigid in its demands.

Truth Is Attained by Experience

Virtue can only be known by doing, and the knowledge of Truth can only be arrived at by perfecting oneself in the practice of Virtue. To be complete in the practice and acquisition of Virtue is to be complete in the knowledge of Truth.

Truth can only be arrived at by daily and hourly

~ Out from the Heart

doing the lessons of Virtue, beginning with the simplest, and passing on to the more difficult. A child patiently and obediently learns his lessons at school by constantly practicing, ever exerting himself until all failures and difficulties are surmounted. Likewise does the child of Truth, undaunted by failure, and made stronger by difficulties, apply himself to rightdoing in thought and action. As he succeeds in acquiring Virtue, his mind unfolds itself in the knowledge of Truth, and it is a knowledge in which he can securely rest.

First Steps in The Higher Life

SEEING THAT THE PATH OF VIRTUE is the Path of Knowledge, and that before the all-embracing Principles of Truth can be comprehended, perfection in the more lowly steps must be acquired, how, then, shall a disciple of Truth begin?

How shall one who aspires to the righting of his mind and the purification of his heart—that heart which is the fountain and repository of all the issues of life—learn the lessons of Virtue? How does he thus build himself up in the strength of knowledge, destroying ignorance and the ills of life? What are the first lessons, the first steps? How are they learned? How are they practiced? How are they mastered and understood?

The first lessons consist in overcoming those wrong mental conditions which are most easily eradicated, and which are the common barriers to spiritual progress, as well as in practicing the simple domestic and social virtues. The reader will be better aided if I group and classify the first ten steps in three lessons as follows:

Vices of the Body to be Overcome and Eradicated
(First Lesson: Discipline of the Body)
1st step: Idleness, Laziness or Indolence
2nd step: Self-Indulgence or Gluttony

Vices of the Tongue to be Overcome and Eradicated
(Second Lesson: Discipline of Speech)
3rd step: Slander
4th step: Gossip and Idle Conversation
5th step: Abusive and Unkind Speech
6th step: Frivolity or Irreverent Speech
7th step: Critical, Captious or Fault-finding Speech

Virtues to be Practiced and Acquired
(Third Lesson: Discipline of Tendencies)
8th step: Unselfish Performance of Duty
9th step: Unswerving Rectitude or Moral Integrity
10th step: Unlimited Forgiveness

The two vices of the body, and the five of the tongue, are so called because they are manifested in the body and tongue. Also, by so definitely classifying them, the mind of the reader will be better helped. But it must be clearly understood that these vices arise primarily in the mind, and are wrong conditions of the heart worked out in the body and the tongue.

The existence of such chaotic conditions is an indication that the mind is altogether unenlightened as to the real meaning and purpose of life, and their eradication is the beginning of a virtuous, steadfast, and enlightened life.

But how shall these vices be overcome and eradicated? By first, and at once, checking and controlling their outward manifestations and by suppressing the wrong act. This will stimulate the mind to watchfulness and reflection until, by repeated practice, it will come to perceive and understand the dark, wrong, and erroneous conditions of mind, out of which such acts spring. It will then abandon them entirely.

The First Step—Overcoming Laziness

It will be seen that the first step in the discipline of the mind is the overcoming of indolence or laziness. This is the easiest step, and until it is perfectly accomplished, the other steps cannot be taken. The clinging to indolence constitutes a complete barrier to the Path of Truth. Indolence consists in giving the body more ease and sleep than it requires, in procrastinating, and in shirking and neglecting those things which should receive immediate attention.

This condition of laziness must be overcome by rousing up the body at an early hour, giving it just the amount of sleep it requires for complete recuperation, and by doing promptly and vigorously, every task, every duty, no matter how small, as it comes along.

On no account should food or drink be taken in bed. And to lie in bed after one has awakened, indulging in ease and reverie, is a habit fatal to promptness and resolution of character, and purity of mind. Nor should one attempt to do his thinking at such a time. Strong, pure, and true thinking is impossible under such circumstances. A man should go to bed to sleep, not to think. He should get up to think and work, not to sleep.

The Second Step—Overcoming Gluttony

The next step is the overcoming of self-indulgence or gluttony. The glutton is he who eats for animal gratification only, without considering the true end and object of eating. He eats more than his body requires, and is greedy after sweet things and rich dishes.

Such undisciplined desire can only be overcome by reducing the quantity of food eaten, and the number of meals per day, and by resorting to a simple and uninvolved diet. Regular hours should be set apart for meals, and eating at other times should be rigidly avoided. Suppers should be abolished, as they are altogether unnecessary, and promote heavy sleep and cloudiness of mind.

The pursuit of such a method of discipline will rapidly bring the once ungoverned appetite under control, and as the sensual sin of self-indulgence is taken out of the mind, the right selection of foods will be instinctively and infallibly adapted to the purified mental condition.

A Change of Heart Most Important

It should be well borne in mind that a change of heart is the needful thing, and that any change of diet which does not promote this end is futile. When one eats for enjoyment, he is gluttonous. The heart must be purified of sensual craving and gustatory lust.

When the body is well controlled and firmly guided; when that which is to be done is done vigorously;

when no task or duty is delayed; when early rising has become a delight; when frugality, simplicity, temperance, and abstinence are firmly established; when one is contented with the food which is put before him, no matter how scanty and plain, and the craving for gustatory pleasure is at an end—then the first two steps in the Higher Life are accomplished. Then is the first great lesson in Truth learned. Thus is established in the heart the foundation of a poised, self-governed, virtuous life.

The Third Step—Overcoming Slanderous Speech

The next lesson is the lesson of Virtuous Speech, in which there are five orderly steps. The first of these is overcoming the habit of slanderous speech. Slander consists of inventing or repeating unkind and evil reports about others, in exposing and magnifying the faults of others, or of absent friends, and in introducing unworthy insinuations. The elements of thoughtlessness, cruelty, insincerity, and untruthfulness enter into every slanderous act.

He who aims at the living of the right life will commence to check the cruel word of slander before it has gone forth from his lips. He will then check and eliminate the insincere thought which gave rise to it.

He will watch that he does not vilify or defame anyone. He will refrain from disparaging, defaming, and condemning the absent friend, whose face he has so recently smiled into or kissed, or whose hand he has shaken. He will not say of another that which he dare not say to his face. Thus, coming at last to think sacredly of the character and reputation of others, he will destroy those wrong conditions of mind which give rise to slander.

The Fourth Step—Overcoming Gossip
The next step is the overcoming of gossip and idle conversation. Idle speech consists in talking about the private affairs of others, in talking merely to pass away the time, and in engaging in aimless and irrelevant conversation. Such an ungoverned condition of speech is the outcome of an ill-regulated mind.

The man of virtue will bridle his tongue, and thus learn how rightly to govern the mind. He will not let his tongue run idly and foolishly, but will make his speech strong and pure, and will either talk with a purpose or remain silent.

The Fifth Step—Overcoming Abusive Speech
Abusive and unkind speech is the next vice to be

overcome. The man who abuses and accuses others has himself wandered far from the Right Way. To hurl hard words and names at others is to sink deeply into folly. When a man is inclined to abuse, curse, and condemn others, let him restrain his tongue and look within himself. The virtuous man refrains from all abusive language and quarreling. He employs only words that are useful, necessary, pure, and true.

The Sixth Step—Overcoming Frivolous Talk

The sixth step is the overcoming of levity, or irreverent speech. Light and frivolous talking; the repeating of crude jokes; the telling of vulgar stories, having no other purpose than to raise an empty laugh; offensive familiarity, and the employment of contemptuous and disrespectful words when speaking to or of others, and particularly of one's elders and those who rank as one's teachers, guardians or superiors—all of this will be put away by the lover of Virtue and Truth.

Upon the altar of irreverence absent friends and companions are immolated for the passing excitement of a momentary laugh, and all the sanctity of life is sacrificed to the zest for ridicule. When respect towards others and the giving of reverence where reverence is due are abandoned, Virtue is abandoned.

The Wisdom of James Allen III ~

When modesty, significance, and dignity are eliminated from speech and behavior, Truth is lost. Yea, even its entrance gate is hidden away and forgotten.

Irreverence is degrading even in the young, but when it accompanies grey hairs, and appears in the demeanor of the preacher—this is indeed a piteous spectacle. And when this can be imitated and followed after, then are the blind leading the blind, then have elders, preachers, and people lost their way.

The virtuous will be of earnest and reverent speech. He will think and speak of the absent as he thinks and speaks of the dead—tenderly and sacredly. He will put away thoughtlessness, and watch that he does not sacrifice his dignity to gratify a passing impulse to frivolity and superficiality. His humor will be pure and innocent, his voice will be subdued and musical, and his soul will be filled with grace and sweetness as he succeeds in conducting himself as becomes a man of Truth.

The Seventh Step—Overcoming Criticism

The last step in the second lesson is the overcoming of criticism, or fault-finding speech. This vice of the tongue consists in magnifying and harping on small or apparent faults, in foolish quibbling and hairsplitting, and in pursuing vain arguments based upon groundless suppositions, beliefs, and opinions.

Life is short and real, and sin, sorrow and pain are not remedied by carping and contention. The man who is ever on the watch to catch at the words of others in order to contradict and dispute them, has yet to reach the higher way of holiness, the truer life of self-surrender. The man who is ever on the alert to check his own words in order to soften and purify them will find the higher way and the truer life. He will conserve his energies, maintain his composure of mind, and preserve within himself the spirit of Truth.

When the tongue is well controlled and wisely subdued; when selfish impulses and unworthy thoughts no longer rush to the tongue demanding utterance; when the speech has become harmless, pure, gentle, gracious, and purposeful, and no word is uttered but in sincerity and honesty—then are the five steps to virtuous speech accomplished, then is the second great lesson in Truth learned and mastered.

The Higher Life Requires Discipline

And now some will ask, "But why all this discipline of the body and restraint of the tongue? Surely the Higher Life can be realized and known without such strenuous labor, such incessant effort and watchfulness?" No, it cannot. In the spiritual as the material, nothing is done without labor, and the higher cannot be known until the lower is fulfilled.

Can a man make a table before he has learned how to handle a tool and drive a nail? And can a man fashion his mind in accordance with Truth before he has overcome the slavery of his body?

As the intricate subtleties of language cannot be understood and wielded before the alphabet and the simplest words are mastered, neither can the deep subtleties of the mind be understood and purified before the A B C of right conduct is perfectly acquired.

As for the labor involved—does not the youth joyfully and patiently submit himself to a seven-years' apprenticeship in order to master a craft? And does he not, day by day, carefully and faithfully carry out every detail of his master's instructions, looking forward to the time when, perfected through obedience and practice, he shall be himself a master?

Where is the man who sincerely aims at excellence in music, painting, literature, or in any trade, business, or profession who is not willing to give his whole life to the acquirement of that particular perfection? Shall labor, then, be considered where the very highest excellence is concerned—the excellence of Truth?

He who says, "The Path which you have pointed out is too difficult; I must have Truth without labor, salvation without effort," that man will not find his way out of the confusions and sufferings of selfhood. He will not find the calm, well-fortified mind and the wisely ordered life. His love is for ease and enjoyment, and not for Truth.

He who, deep in his heart, adores Truth, and aspires to know it, will consider no labor too great to be undertaken, but will adopt it joyfully and pursue it patiently. By perseverance in practice he will come to the knowledge of Truth.

The End of Evil Leads to Good

The necessity for this preliminary discipline of the body and tongue will be more clearly perceived when it is fully understood that all these wrong outward conditions are merely the expressions of wrong conditions of the heart. An indolent body means an indolent mind; an ill-regulated tongue reveals an ill-regulated mind, and the process of remedying the manifested condition is really a method of rectifying the inward state.

Moreover, the overcoming of these conditions is

only a small part of what is really involved in the process. The ceasing from evil leads to, and is inseparably connected with, the practice of good. While a man is overcoming laziness and self-indulgence, he is really cultivating and developing the virtues of abstinence, temperance, punctuality, and self-denial. He is acquiring the strength, energy, and resolve which are indispensable to the successful accomplishment of the higher tasks. While he is overcoming the vices of speech, he is developing the virtues of truthfulness, sincerity, reverence, kindliness, and self-control, and is gaining that mental steadiness and fixedness of purpose, without which the more remote subtleties of the mind cannot be regulated, and the higher stages of conduct and enlightenment cannot be reached.

Also, as he has to do right, his knowledge deepens, and his insight is intensified. Just as a child's heart is glad when a school task is mastered, so with each victory achieved, the man of virtue experiences a bliss which the seeker after pleasure and excitement can never know.

The Third Lesson—Striving for Virtue

And now we come to the third lesson in the Higher Life, which consists of practicing and mastering, in one's daily life, three great fundamental Virtues:

1) Unselfish Performance of Duty
2) Unswerving Rectitude (Moral Integrity)
3) Unlimited Forgiveness

Having prepared the mind by overcoming the more surface and chaotic conditions mentioned in the first two lessons, the striver after Virtue and Truth is now ready to enter upon greater and more difficult tasks, and to control and purify the deeper motives of the heart.

The Eighth Step—Unselfish Duty

Without the right performance of duty, the higher virtues cannot be known, and Truth cannot be apprehended. Duty is generally regarded as an irksome labor, a compulsory something which must be toiled through, or be in some way avoided. This way of regarding duty proceeds from a selfish condition of mind, and a wrong understanding of life. All duty should be regarded as sacred, and its faithful and unselfish performance one of the leading rules of conduct.

All personal and selfish considerations should be extracted and cast away from the doing of one's duty, and when this is done, duty ceases to be irksome, and becomes joyful. Duty is only irksome to him who craves some selfish enjoyment or benefit for himself. Let the man who is chafing under the irksomeness of his duty look to himself, and he will find that his wearisomeness proceeds, not from the duty itself, but from his selfish desire to escape it.

He who neglects duty, be it great or small, or of a public or private nature, neglects Virtue. He who in his heart rebels against duty, rebels against Virtue. When Duty becomes a thing of love, and when every particular duty is done accurately, faithfully, and dispassionately, there is much subtle selfishness removed from the heart, and a great step is taken towards the heights of Truth. The virtuous man concentrates his mind on the perfect doing of his own duty, and does not interfere with the duty of another.

The Ninth Step—Unswerving Rectitude

The ninth step is the practice of Unswerving Rectitude or Moral Integrity. This Virtue must be firmly established in the mind, and so enter into every detail of a man's life. All dishonesty, deception, trickery, and misrepresentation must be forever put away, and the heart purged of every vestige of insincerity and

~ Out from the Heart

deception. The least digression from the path of rectitude or righteousness is a deviation from Virtue.

There must be no extravagance and exaggeration of speech, but the simple truth should be stated. Engaging in deception, no matter how apparently insignificant, for boastful pride, or with the hope of personal advantage, is a state of delusion which one should make efforts to dispel. It is demanded of the man of Virtue that he shall not only practice the most rigid honesty in thought, word, and deed, but that he shall be exact in his statements, omitting and adding nothing to the actual truth

In thus shaping his mind to the principle of Rectitude or moral integrity, he will gradually come to deal with people and things in a just and impartial spirit, considering equity before himself, and viewing all things with freedom from personal bias, passion, and prejudice. When the Virtue of Rectitude is fully practiced and comprehended, so that all temptation to untruthfulness and insincerity has ceased, then is the heart made purer and nobler. Then is character strengthened, and knowledge enlarged, and life takes on a new meaning and a new power. Thus is the ninth step accomplished.

The Tenth Step—Unlimited Forgiveness

The tenth step is the practice of Unlimited Forgiveness. This consists in overcoming the sense of injury which springs from vanity, selfishness and pride; and in exercising disinterested charity and large-heartedness towards all. Spite, retaliation, and revenge are so utterly ignoble, so base, and so small and foolish, as to be altogether unworthy of being noticed or harbored. No one who fosters such conditions in his heart can lift himself above folly and suffering, and guide his life aright. Only by casting them away, and ceasing to be moved by them, can a man's eyes be opened to the true way of life. Only by developing a forgiving and charitable spirit can he hope to approach and perceive the strength and beauty of a well-ordered life.

In the heart of the strongly virtuous man, no feeling of personal injury can arise. He has put away all retaliation, and has no enemies. If other men should regard themselves as his enemies, he will regard them kindly, understanding their ignorance, and making full allowance for it.

When this state of heart is arrived at, then the tenth step in the discipline of one's self-seeking inclinations is accomplished. Then the third great lesson

~ Out from the Heart

in Virtue and Knowledge is learned and mastered.

The Beginning Steps Are Easiest

Having thus laid down the first ten steps and three lessons in right-doing and right-knowing, I leave those of my readers who are prepared for them to learn and master them in their everyday life.

There is, of course, a still higher discipline of the body, a more far-reaching discipline of the tongue, and greater and more all-embracing virtues to acquire and understand before the highest state of bliss and knowledge can be grasped. But it is not my purpose to deal with them here. I have expounded only the first and easiest lessons on the Higher Path, and by the time these are thoroughly mastered, the reader will have become so purified, strengthened, and enlightened, that he will not be left in the dark as to his future progress.

Those of my readers who have completed these three lessons will already have perceived, beyond and above, the high altitudes of Truth, and the narrow and precipitous track which leads to them, and will choose whether they shall proceed.

The straight Path which I have laid down can be pursued by all with greater profit to themselves and to the world. And even those who do not aspire to the attainment of Truth, will develop greater intellectual and moral strength, finer judgement, and deeper peace of mind by perfecting themselves in this Path.

Nor will their material prosperity suffer by this change of heart; nay, it will be rendered truer, purer, and more enduring. For if there is one who is capable of succeeding and fitted to achieve, it is the man who has abandoned the petty weaknesses and everyday vices of his kind, who is strong enough to rule his body and mind, and who pursues with fixed resolve the path of unswerving integrity and sterling virtue.

Mental Conditions and Their Effects

WITHOUT GOING into the details of the greater steps and lessons in the right life (a task outside the scope of this small work) a few hints concerning those mental conditions from which life in its totality springs seem in order. These hints will prove helpful to those who are ready and willing to penetrate further into the inner realm of heart and mind where Love, Wisdom, and Peace await the rapidly progressing student of life.

All sin is ignorance. It is a condition of darkness and undevelopment. The wrong-thinker and the wrong-doer is in the same position in the school of life as the ignorant pupil in the school of learning. He has yet to learn how to think and act correctly, that is, in accordance with Law. The pupil in learning is not happy so long as he does his lessons wrongly. Likewise, unhappiness cannot be escaped while sin remains unconquered.

All Suffering Is Rooted in Error

Life is a series of lessons. Some are diligent in learning them, and they become pure, wise, and altogether happy. Others are negligent, and do not apply themselves. They remain impure, foolish, and unhappy.

Every form of unhappiness springs from a wrong condition of mind. Happiness is inherent in right conditions of mind. Happiness is mental harmony; unhappiness is mental inharmony. While a man lives in wrong conditions of mind, he will live a wrong life, and will suffer continually.

Suffering is rooted in error. Bliss is inherent in enlightenment. There is salvation for man only in the destruction of his own ignorance, error, and self-delusion. Where there are wrong conditions of mind there is bondage and unrest. Where there are right conditions of mind there is freedom and peace.

Ten Wrong Mental Conditions and Their Effects

Here are some of the leading wrong mental conditions and their disastrous effects upon one's life:

~ Out from the Heart

1. *Hatred*—which leads to injury, violence, disaster, and suffering.

2. *Lust*—which leads to confusion of intellect, remorse, shame, and wretchedness.

3. *Covetousness*—which leads to fear, unrest, unhappiness, and loss.

4. *Pride*—which leads to disappointment, humiliation, and lack of self-knowledge.

5. *Vanity*—which leads to distress and mortification of spirit.

6. *Condemnation*—which leads to persecution and hatred from others.

7. *Ill-will*—which leads to failures and troubles.

8. *Self-indulgence*—which leads to misery, loss of judgement, grossness, disease, and neglect.

9. *Anger*—which leads to the loss of power and influence.

10. *Desire* or *Self-slavery*—which leads to grief, folly, sorrow, uncertainty, and loneliness.

The above wrong conditions of mind are merely negations. They are states of darkness and deprivation and not of positive power. Evil is not a power; it is ignorance and misuse of good. The hater is he who has failed to do the lesson of Love correctly, and he suffers in consequence. When he succeeds in doing it rightly, the hatred will have disappeared, and he will see and understand the darkness and impotence of hatred. This is so with every wrong condition.

Ten Right Mental Conditions and Their Effects

The following are some of the more important right mental conditions and their beneficial effects upon one's life:

1. *Love*—which leads to gentle conditions, bliss, and blessedness.
2. *Purity*—which leads to intellectual clearness, joy, invincible confidence.
3. *Selflessness*—which leads to courage, satisfaction, happiness, and abundance.
4. *Humility*—which leads to calmness, restfulness, knowledge of Truth.
5. *Gentleness*—which leads to emotional equilibrium, contentment under all circumstances.
6. *Compassion*—which leads to protection, love, and reverence from others.
7. *Goodwill*—which leads to gladness, success.
8. *Self-control*—which leads to peace of mind, true judgement, refinement, health, and honor.

~ Out from the Heart

9. *Patience*—which leads to mental power, far-reaching influence.

10. *Self-conquest*—which leads to enlightenment, wisdom, insight, and profound peace.

Striving for Right Mental Conditions

The above right conditions of mind are states of positive power, light, joyful possession, and knowledge. The good man *knows*. He has learned to do his lessons correctly, and thereby understands the exact proportions which make up the sum of life. He is enlightened, and he knows good and evil. He is supremely happy, doing only that which is divinely right.

The man who is involved in the wrong conditions of mind, does not know. He is ignorant of good and evil, of himself, of the inward causes which make his life. He is unhappy, and believes other people are entirely the cause of his unhappiness. He works blindly, and lives in darkness, seeing no central purpose in existence, and no orderly and lawful sequence in the course of things.

He who aspires to the attainment of the Higher Life in its completion—who would perceive with unveiled vision the true order of things and the meaning of life—let him abandon all the wrong conditions of the heart, and persevere unceasingly in the practice of good. If he suffers, or doubts, or is unhappy, let him search within until he finds the cause, and having found it, let him cast it away. Let him so guard and purify his heart that every day less of evil and more of good shall issue therefrom. So he will daily become stronger, nobler, and wiser. So will his blessedness increase, and the Light of Truth, growing ever brighter and brighter within him, will dispel all gloom, and illuminate his Pathway.

Exhortation

DISCIPLES OF TRUTH, lovers of Virtue, seekers of Wisdom; you, also, who are sorrow stricken, knowing the emptiness of the self-life, and who aspire to the life that is supremely beautiful, and serenely joyful—take now yourselves in hand, enter the Door of Discipline, and know the Better Life.

Put away self-delusion. Behold yourself as you are, and see the Path of Virtue as it is. There is no lazy way to Truth. He who would stand upon the mountain's summit must strenuously climb, and must rest only to gather strength. But if the climbing is less glorious than the cloudless summit, it is still glorious. Discipline in itself is beautiful, and the end result of discipline is sweet.

The Wisdom of James Allen III ~

Truth Is Only Reached by Discipline

Rise early and meditate. Begin each day with a conquered body, and a mind fortified against error and weakness. Temptation will never be overcome by unprepared fighting. The mind must be armed and arrayed in the silent hour. It must be trained to perceive, to know, to understand. Sin and temptation disappear when right understanding is developed.

Right understanding is reached through unabated discipline. Truth cannot be reached but through discipline. Patience will increase by effort and practice, and patience will make discipline beautiful.

Discipline is irksome to the impatient man and the lover of self, so he avoids it, and continues to live loosely and confusedly.

Discipline is not irksome to the lover of Truth, and he will find the infinite patience which can wait, work, and overcome. Just as the joy of the gardener who sees his or her flowers develop day by day, so is the joy of the man of discipline who sees the divine flowers of Purity, Wisdom, Compassion, and Love, grow within his heart.

First Weakness, Then Strength

The loose-liver cannot escape sorrow and pain.

~ Out from the Heart

The undisciplined mind falls, weak and helpless, before the fierce onslaught of passion.

Array well your mind, then, lover of Truth. Be watchful, thoughtful, and resolute. Your salvation is at hand; your readiness and effort are all that are needed. If you fail ten times, do not be disheartened. If you should fail a hundred times, rise up and pursue your way. If you should fail a thousand times, do not despair. When the right Path is entered, success is sure if the Path is not utterly abandoned

First strife, and then victory. First labor, and then rest. First weakness, and then strength. In the beginning the lower life, and the glare and confusion of battle, and at the end the Life Beautiful, the Silence, and the Peace.

All common things, each day's events,
That with the hour begin and end;
Our pleasures and our discontents
Are rounds by which we may ascend.
We have not wings, we cannot soar;
But we have feet to scale and climb.
—*Longfellow*

BOOK TWO

Byways of Blessedness

Byways of Blessedness
Table of Contents

Foreword..65

Right Beginnings..67

Small Tasks and Duties..78

Transcending Difficulties and Perplexities..............92

Burden-Dropping..102

Hidden Sacrifices...116

Sympathy...134

Forgiveness..151

Seeing No Evil...162

Abiding Joy..188

Silentness...196

Solitude..207

Standing Alone..220

Understanding The Simple Laws of Life..............228

Happy Endings..244

Foreword

ALONG THE HIGHWAYS of Burma there are placed, at regular distances away from the dust of the road and under the cool shade of groups of trees, small wooden buildings called "rest-houses," where the weary traveler may rest awhile, and allay his thirst and assuage his hunger and fatigue by partaking of the food and water that the kindly inhabitants place there as religious duty.

Along the great highways of life there are such resting-places. Away from the heat of passion and the dust of disappointment, under the cool and refreshing shade of lowly Wisdom, are the humble, unimposing "rest-houses" of peace, and the little, almost unnoticed, byways of blessedness, where alone the weary and footsore can find strength and healing.

Nor can these byways be ignored without suffering. Along the great road of life, hurrying and eager to reach some illusive goal, presses the multitude. They despise the apparently insignificant "rest-houses" of true thought, not heeding the narrow little byways of blessed action, which are regarded by them as unimportant. And hour by hour men are fainting and falling, and numbers that cannot be counted perish of heart-hunger, heart-thirst, and heart-fatigue.

But he who will step aside from the passionate press, and deign to enter the byways presented here, his happy feet shall press the incomparable flowers of blessedness, his eyes will be gladdened with their beauty, and his mind refreshed with their sweet perfume. Rested and sustained, he shall escape the fever and delirium of life, and, strong and happy, he will not fall fainting in the dust nor perish by the way, but will successfully accomplish his journey.

—*James Allen*

Right Beginnings

LIFE IS FULL OF BEGINNINGS. They are presented every day and every hour to every person. Most beginnings are small and appear trivial and insignificant, but in reality they are the most important things in life.

See how in the material world everything proceeds from small beginnings. The mightiest river is at first a stream over which the grasshopper could leap. The great flood starts with a few drops of rain. The sturdy oak, which has endured the storms of a thousand winters, was once an acorn.

Consider how in the spiritual world the greatest things proceed from smallest beginnings. A light fancy may be the inception of a wonderful invention or an immortal work of art. A spoken sentence may turn the tide of history. A pure thought entertained may lead to the exercise of a world-wide regenerative power.

Have you yet discovered the vast importance of beginnings? Do you really know what is involved in a beginning? Do you know the number of beginnings you are continuously making, and do you realize their full importance? If not, come with me for a short time, thoughtfully to explore this much ignored byway of blessedness. For blessed it is when wisely resorted to, and much strength and comfort it holds for the understanding mind.

Beginnings Presuppose an Ending

A beginning is a cause, and as such it must be followed by an effect, or a train of effects, and the effect will always be of the same nature as the cause. The nature of an initial impulse determines the body of its results. A beginning also presupposes an ending, a consummation, achievement, or goal. A gate leads to a path, and the path leads to some particular destination. So a beginning leads to results, and results lead to a completion.

There are right beginnings and wrong beginnings, followed by effects of a like nature. You can, by careful thought, avoid wrong beginnings and make right begin-

~ Byways of Blessedness

nings, and so escape evil results and enjoy good results.

There are beginnings over which you have no control and authority. These are outside of you, in the universe, in the world of nature around you, and in other people possessing the same liberty as yourself.

Do not concern yourself with these beginnings, but direct your energies and attention to those beginnings over which you have complete control and authority, those which bring about the complicated web of results which compose your life. These beginnings are to be found in the realm of your own thoughts and actions; in your mental attitude toward the variety of circumstances through which you pass; in your conduct day by day—in short, in your life as you make it, which is your world of good or ill.

Beginning The Day Right

In aiming at the life of Blessedness one of the simplest beginnings to be considered and rightly made is that which we all make every day—the beginning of each day's life.

How do you begin each day? At what hour do you rise? How do you begin your work? In what frame of mind do you enter upon the sacred life of a new day? What answer can you give your heart to these impor-

The Wisdom of James Allen III ~

tant questions? You will find that much happiness or unhappiness follows upon the right or wrong beginning of the day, and that, when every day is wisely begun, happy and harmonious sequences will mark its course, and life in its totality will not fall far short of the ideal blessedness.

It is a right and strong beginning to the day to rise at an early hour. Even if your worldly work does not demand it, it is wise to make of it a habit, and begin the day strongly by shaking off indolence and by putting on vigor and energy. How are you to develop strength of will, mind, and body if you begin every day by yielding to weakness?

Self-indulgence is followed by unhappiness. Those who lie in bed till late are not necessarily bright, cheerful, and fresh, but are often the prey of irritabilities, depressions, debilities, nervous disorders, abnormal fancies, and all unhappy moods. This is the heavy price they have to pay for their daily indulgence.

Yet, so blinding is the pandering to self that, like the man who takes his daily dram in the belief that it is bracing his nerves, which it is all the time shattering, so the lie-a-bed is convinced that long hours of ease are necessary for him as a possible remedy for those very moods, weaknesses, and disorders of which his indulgence is the cause. Men and women are unaware of the great losses that they entail by this common indulgence: loss of strength both of mind and body, loss of prosperity, loss of knowledge, and loss of happiness.

Early to Rise

Begin the day by rising early. If you have no object in doing so, never mind. Arise, go out for a gentle walk among the beauties of nature, and you will experience a buoyancy, a freshness, and a delight, as well as a peace of mind, that will reward you for your effort.

One good effort is followed by another. When a man begins the day by rising early, even though with no other purpose in view, he will find the silent early hour conducive to clearness of mind and calmness of thought. His early morning walk will be profitable in enabling him to become an orderly thinker, and so to see life and its problems, as well as himself and his affairs, in a clearer light. In time, he will rise early for the express purpose of preparing and harmonizing his mind to meet any and every difficulty with wisdom and calm strength.

There is, indeed, so spiritual an influence in the early morning hour, so divine a silence and inexpressible a repose, that he who, purposeful and strong, throws off the mantle of ease and climbs the hills to greet the morning sun will thereby climb a considerable distance up the hills of blessedness and truth.

The right beginning of the day will be followed by cheerfulness at the first meal, permeating the household with a sunny influence. Then the work of the day will be undertaken in a strong and confident spirit, and the whole day will be well lived.

There is also a sense in which every day will be regarded as the beginning of a new life, in which one can think, act, and live newly, and in a wiser and better spirit.

Each Day Is a Fresh Beginning

"Every day is a fresh beginning;
Every morn is the world made new,
Ye who are weary of sorrow and sinning,
Here is a beautiful hope for you,
A hope for me and a hope for you."

Do not dwell upon the sins and mistakes of yesterday so exclusively as to have no energy and mind left for living rightly today, and do not think that the sins of yesterday can prevent you from living right today. Begin today right with the world, and, aided by the accumulated experiences of all your past days, live it better than any of your previous days; for you cannot possibly live it better unless you begin it better. The character of the whole day depends upon the way it is begun.

Another beginning of great importance is the beginning of any particular and responsible undertaking. How does a man begin the building of a house? He first secures a plan of the proposed edifice and proceeds to build according to the plan, scrupulously following it in every detail, from the foundation up. Should he neglect the beginning—the obtaining of an architectural plan—his labor would be wasted, and his building, should it reach completion without tumbling to pieces, would be insecure and worthless.

The same law holds good in any important work. The right beginning and first essential is a definite mental plan on which to build. Nature will have no slipshod work, no slovenliness, and she annihilates confusion, or rather, confusion is in itself annihilation. Order, definiteness, and purpose, eternally and universally prevail; and he who in his operations ignores these elements of precision at once deprives himself of substantiality, completeness, and success.

The Wisdom of James Allen III ~

Success Depends Upon an Orderly Plan

"Life without a plan,
As useless as the moment it began,
Serves merely as a soil for discontent
To thrive in, an encumbrance ere half spent."

Let a man start in business without having in his mind a well formed plan to systematically pursue, and he will be incoherent in his efforts and will fail in his business operations. The laws to be observed in the building of a house also operate in the building up of a business. A definite plan is followed by coherent effort; and coherent effort is followed by well-knit and orderly results—completeness, perfection, success, and happiness.

But not only mechanical and commercial enterprise—all undertakings, of whatever nature, come under this law. The author's book, the artist's picture, the orator's speech, the reformer's work, the inventor's machine, the general's campaign, are all carefully planned in the mind before the attempt to actualize them is commenced. And in accordance with the unity, solidarity, and perfection of the original mental plan will be the actual and ultimate success of the undertaking.

Successful men, influential men, and good men are

those who, among other things, have learned the value and utilized the power hidden in the obscure beginnings that the foolish man passes by as insignificant.

But the most important beginning of all—that upon which blessedness inevitably depends, yet the one most neglected and least understood—is the inception of thought in the hidden, but causal region of the mind.

All Conduct Molded by Thought

Your whole life is a series of effects having their cause in thought—in your own thought. All conduct is made and molded by thought; all deeds, good or bad, are thoughts made visible. A seed put into the ground is the beginning of a plant or tree. The seed germinates, the plant or tree comes forth into the light and evolves. A thought put into the mind is the beginning of a line of conduct: the thought first sends down its roots into the mind, then pushes forth into the light in the form of actions or conduct, which evolve into character and destiny.

Loving, gentle, kind, unselfish, and pure thoughts are right beginnings, leading to blissful results. This is so simple, so plain, so absolutely true; and yet how neglected, how evaded, and how little understood!

Gardening Your Mind

The gardener who most carefully studies how, when, and where to put in his seeds gains the greater horticultural knowledge and obtains the best results. The best crops gladden the soul of him who makes the best beginning. The man who most patiently studies how to put into his mind the seeds of strong, wholesome, and charitable thoughts, will obtain the best results in life, and gain the greater knowledge of truth. The greatest blessedness comes to him who infuses into his mind the purest and noblest thoughts.

None but right acts can follow right thoughts. None but a right life can follow right acts—and by living a right life all blessedness is achieved.

He who considers the nature and import of his thoughts, who strives daily to eliminate bad thoughts and supplant them with good, comes at last to see that thoughts are the beginnings of results which affect every fiber of his being, which potently influence every event and circumstance of his life. When he thus sees, he thinks only right thoughts, and he chooses to make only those mental beginnings which lead to peace and blessedness.

Wrong thoughts are painful in their inception, painful in their growth, and painful in their fruitage.

Right thoughts are blissful in their inception, blissful in their growth, and blissful in their fruitage.

Many are the right beginnings which a person must discover and adopt on his way to wisdom. But that which is first and last, most important and all embracing, which is the source and fountain of all abiding happiness, is the right beginning of the mental operations—this implies the steady development of self-control, will-power, steadfastness, strength, purity, gentleness, insight, and comprehension. It leads to the perfecting of life, for he who thinks perfectly has abolished all unhappiness. His every moment is peaceful. His years are rounded with bliss—he has attained complete and perfect blessedness.

> *For common life its wants*
> *And ways, would I set forth in beauteous hues.*
> —*Browning*

Small Tasks and Duties

AS PAIN AND BLISS inevitably follow wrong and right beginnings, so unhappiness and blessedness are inseparably bound up with small tasks and duties. Not that a duty has any power of itself to bestow happiness or the reverse—this is contained in the attitude of mind which is assumed towards the duty—and everything depends upon the way in which it is approached and done.

Not only great happiness but great power arises from doing little things unselfishly, wisely, and perfectly, for life in its totality is made up of little things. Wisdom inheres in the common details of everyday existence, and when the parts are made perfect the Whole will be without blemish.

Everything in the universe is made up of little things, and the perfection of the great is based upon the perfection of the small. If any detail of the universe were imperfect the Whole would be imperfect. If any particle were omitted the aggregate would cease to be. Without a grain of dust there could be no world, and the world is perfect because the grain of dust is perfect. Neglect of the small is confusion of the great. The snowflake is as perfect as the star. The dew drop is as symmetrical as the planet. The microbe is not less mathematically proportioned than the man. By laying stone upon stone, plumbing and fitting each with perfect adjustment, the temple at last stands forth in all its architectural beauty. The small precedes the great. The small is not merely the apologetic attendant of the great, it is its master and informing genius.

Greatness Sacrifices Ambition

Vain men are ambitious to be great. They look about to do some great thing, ignoring and despising the little tasks which call for immediate attention, and in the doing of which there is no vainglory. They regard such "trivialities" as beneath the notice of great men. The fool lacks knowledge because he lacks humility, and, inflated with the thought of self-importance, he aims at impossible things.

The great man has become such by the scrupulous and unselfish attention which he has given to small duties. He has become wise and powerful by sacrificing ambition and pride in the doing of those necessary things which evoke no applause and promise no reward. He never sought greatness. He sought faithfulness, unselfishness, integrity, truth; and in finding these in the common round of small tasks and duties he unconsciously ascended to the level of greatness.

The great man knows the vast value that inheres in moments, words, greetings, meals, apparel, correspondence, rest, work, detached efforts, fleeting obligations, in the thousand-and-one little things which press upon him for attention—briefly, in the common details of life. He sees everything as divinely apportioned, needing only the application of dispassionate thought and action on his part to render life blessed and perfect.

The great man neglects nothing and does not hurry. He seeks to escape nothing but error and folly. He attends to every duty as it is presented to him, and does not postpone and regret. By giving himself unreservedly to his nearest duty, forgetting pleasure and pain alike, he attains to that combined childlike simplicity and unconscious power which is greatness.

Greatness Evolves Slowly as a Flower

The advice of Confucius to his disciples: "Eat at your own table as you would at the table of a king," emphasizes the immeasurable importance of little things.

So also does that aphorism of another great teacher, Buddha: "If anything is to be done, let a man do it, let him attack it vigorously." To neglect small tasks, or to execute them in a perfunctory or slovenly manner, is a mark of weakness and folly.

The giving of one's entire and unselfish attention to every duty in its proper place evolves, by a natural growth, higher and ever higher combinations of duties, because it evolves power and develops talent, genius, goodness, and character. A man ascends into greatness as naturally and unconsciously as the plant evolves a flower, and in the same manner, by fitting, with unabated energy and diligence, every effort and detail in its proper place, thus harmonizing life and character without friction or waste of power.

Of the almost innumerable recipes for the development of "will-power" and "concentration" which are now scattered abroad, one looks almost in vain for any wholesome hint applicable to vital experience. "Breathings," "postures," "visualizings," and "occult methods" are practices as delusive as they are artificial and remote from all that is real and essential in life. Whereas the true path—the path of duty, of earnest and undivided application to one's daily task—along which alone will-power and concentration of thought can be wholesomely and normally developed, remains unknown, untrodden, and unexplored even by the elect.

All unnatural forcing and straining in order to gain "power" should be abandoned. There is no way from childhood to adulthood but by growth. Nor is there any other way from folly to wisdom, from ignorance to knowledge, from weakness to strength. A man must learn how to grow little by little, and day after day, by adding thought to thought, effort to effort, and deed to deed.

The True Master

It is true the fakir gains some sort of power by his long persistence in "postures" and "mortifications," but it is a power which is bought at a heavy price. That price is an equal loss of strength in another direction. He is never a strong, useful character, but a mere fantastic specialist in some psychological trick. He is not a developed man, he is a maimed man.

True will-power consists in overcoming the irritabilities, follies, rash impulses, and moral lapses which accompany the daily life of the individual, and which are apt to manifest themselves on every slight provocation. It also consists in developing calmness, self-possession, and dispassionate action in the press and heat of worldly duties, and in the midst of the passionate and unbalanced throng. Anything short of this is not true power, and this can only be developed along the normal pathway of steady growth, in executing ever more and more masterfully, unselfishly, and perfectly one's daily round of legitimate tasks and pressing obligations.

The master is not he whose "psychological accomplishments," rounded by mystery and wonder, leave him in unguarded moments the prey of irritability, regret, peevishment, or other petty folly or vice. The master is he whose "mastery" is manifested in fortitude, non-resentment, steadfastness, calmness, and infinite patience. The true Master is master of himself; anything other than this is not mastery but delusion.

Immerse Yourself in Your Work

The man who sets his whole mind on the doing of each task as it is presented, who puts into it energy and intelligence, shutting all else out from his mind, and striving to do that one thing, no matter how small, completely and perfectly, detaching himself from all reward in his task—that man will every day be acquiring greater command over his mind, and will, by ever-ascending degrees, become at last a man of power—a Master.

Put yourself unreservedly into your present task, and so work, so act, so live that you shall leave each task a finished piece of labor—this is the true way to the acquisition of will-power, concentration of thought, and conservation of energy. Look not about for magical formulas, nor for strained and artificial methods. Every resource is already with you and within you. You have but to learn how wisely to apply yourself in that place which you now occupy. Until this is done those other and higher places which are waiting for you cannot be taken possession of, cannot be reached.

Strength Is Gained by Being Strong

There is no way to strength and wisdom but by acting strongly and wisely in the present moment, and each present moment reveals its own task. The great man, the wise man, does small things greatly, regarding nothing that is necessary as "trivial".

The weak man, the foolish man, does small things carelessly, and meanly. All the while he hankers after some greater work for which, in his neglect and inability in small matters, he is ceaselessly advertising his incapacity. The man who least governs himself is always more ambitious to govern others and assume important responsibilities.

"Whoso neglects a thing which he suspects he ought to do because it seems too small a thing is deceiving himself. It is not too little but too great for him that he doeth it not."

And just as the strong doing of small tasks leads to greater strength, so the doing of those tasks weakly leads to greater weakness. What a man is in his fractional duties that he is in the aggregate of his character. Weakness is as great a source of suffering as sin, and there can be no true blessedness until some measure of strength of character is evolved. The weak man becomes strong by attaching value to little things and doing them accordingly. The strong man becomes weak by falling into looseness and neglect concerning small things, thereby forfeiting his simple wisdom and squandering his energy.

The Law of Growth

Herein we see the beneficent operation of that law of growth which is expressed in the little understood words: "To him that hath shall be given, and from him that hath not shall be taken away even that which he hath."

Man instantly gains or loses by every thought he thinks, every word he says, every act he does, and every work to which he puts hand and heart.

His character, from moment to moment, is a graduating quantity, to or from which some measure of good is added or subtracted during every moment. The gain or loss is involved, even to absoluteness, in each thought, word, and deed as these follow each other in rapid sequence.

He who masters the small becomes the rightful possessor of the great. He who is mastered by the small can achieve no superlative victory.

Life is a kind of cooperative trust in which the whole is of the nature of, and dependent upon, the unit. A successful business, a perfect machine, a glorious temple, or a beautiful character is evolved from the perfect adjustment of a multiplicity of parts.

The Folly of The Fool

The foolish man thinks that little faults, little indulgences, little sins, are of no consequence. He persuades himself that so long as he does not commit flagrant immoralities, he is virtuous, and even holy. But he is thereby deprived of virtue and holiness, and the world knows him accordingly. It does not revere, adore, and love him; it passes him by. He is reckoned of no account; his influence is destroyed. The efforts of such a man to make the world virtuous, his warnings to his fellow-men to abandon great vices, are empty of substance and barren of fruitage.

The insignificance which he attaches to his small vices permeates his whole character and is the measure of his manhood: he is regarded as an insignificant man. The levity with which he commits his errors and publishes his weakness comes back to him in the form of neglect, and loss of influence and respect. He is not sought after, for who will seek to be taught of folly? His work does not prosper, for who will lean upon a reed? His words fall upon deaf ears, for they are void of practice, wisdom, and experience, and who will go after an echo?

The wise man, or he who is becoming wise, sees the danger which lurks in those common personal faults, which men mostly commit thoughtlessly and with impunity. He also sees the salvation which inheres in the abandonment of those faults, as well as in the practice of virtuous thoughts and acts, which the majority disregard as unimportant, and in those quiet but momentous daily conquests over self which are hidden from other's eyes.

Little Things Are Important

He who regards his smallest delinquencies as of the gravest nature, becomes a saint. He sees the far reaching influence, good or bad, which extends from his every thought and act, and how he himself is made or unmade by the soundness or unsoundness of those innumerable details of conduct, which combine to form his character and life. And so he watches, guards, purifies, and perfects himself little by little and step by step.

As the ocean is composed of drops, the earth of grains, and the stars of points of light, so is life composed of thoughts and acts. Without these, life would not be. Every man's life, therefore, is what his apparently detached thoughts and acts make it. Their combination is himself. As the year consists of a given number of sequential moments, so a man's character and life consists of a given number of sequential thoughts and deeds, and the finished whole will bear the imprint of the parts.

"All sorts of things and weather

Must be taken in together,
To make up a year
And a sphere."

Little kindnesses, generosities, and sacrifices make up a kind and generous character. Little renunciations, endurances, and victories over self make up a strong and noble character. The truly honest man is honest in the minutest details of his life. The noble man is noble in every little thing he says and does.

Truth Is Wrapped in Details

It is a fatal delusion with men to think that life is detached from the momentary thought and act, and not to understand that the passing thought and deed is the foundation and substance of life. When this is fully understood all things are seen as sacred, and every act becomes religious. Truth is wrapped up in infinitesimal details. Thoroughness is genius.

"Possessions vanish, and opinions change,
And passions hold a fluctuating seat:
But, by the storms of circumstance unshaken,
And subject neither to eclipse nor wane,
Duty exists."

You do not live your life in the whole; you live it in the fragments and from these the whole emerges. You can resolve to live each fragment nobly if you choose, and, this being done, there can be no particle of baseness in the finished whole. The saying "Take care of your pennies and the dollars will take care of themselves" is seen to be more than worldly-wise when applied spiritually. For, to take care of the present, passing action, knowing that by so doing the total sum and amount of life and character will be safely preserved, is to be divinely wise.

Remain Humble and Be Noble

Do not long to do great and laudable things; these will do themselves if you do your present task nobly. Do not chafe or be irritated at the restrictions and limitations of your present duty, but be nobly unselfish in the doing of it. Put aside discontent, listlessness, and the foolish contemplation of great deeds which lie beyond you—and lo! already the greatness for which you sighed begins to appear. There is no weakness like peevishness or discontentment. Aspire to the attainment of inward nobility, not outward glory, and begin to attain it where you are now.

The irksomeness and sting which you feel to be in

your task are in your mind only. Alter your attitude of mind towards it, and at once the crooked path is made straight, the unhappiness is turned into joy.

See that your every fleeting moment is strong, pure, and purposeful. Put earnestness and unselfishness into every passing task and duty. Make your every thought, word, and deed sweet and true. Thus learning, by practice and experience, the inestimable value of the small things of life, you will gather, little by little, abundant and enduring blessedness.

"Wrapped in our nearest duty is the key
  Which shall unlock for us the Heavenly Gate:
Unveiled, the Heavenly Vision he shall see,
  Who cometh not too early or too late."

> *"Like the star*
> *That shines afar,*
> *Without haste*
> *And without rest.*
> *Let each man wheel with steady sway*
> *Round the task that rules the day,*
>   *And do his best."*
>   —*Goethe*

Transcending Difficulties and Perplexities

TO SUGGEST THAT ANY DEGREE of blessedness may be extracted from difficulties and perplexities will doubtless appear absurd to many. But truth is ever paradoxical, and the curses of the foolish are the blessings of the wise. Difficulties arise in ignorance and weakness, and they call for the attainment of knowledge and the acquisition of strength.

As understanding is acquired by right living, difficulties become fewer, and perplexities gradually fade away, like the perishable mists which they are. Your difficulty is not contained, primarily, in the situation which gave rise to it, but in the mental state with which you regard that situation and which you bring to bear upon it.

That which is difficult to a child presents no difficulty to the matured mind of the man; and that which to the mind of an unintelligent man is surrounded with perplexity would afford no ground for perplexity to an intelligent man.

To the untutored and undeveloped mind of the child, how great, and apparently insurmountable, appear the difficulties which are involved in the learning of some simple lesson. How many anxious and laborious hours and days, or even months, its solution costs. And, frequently, how many tears are shed in hopeless contemplation of the unmastered, and apparently insurmountable, wall of difficulty! Yet the difficulty is in the ignorance of the child only. Its conquest and solution is absolutely necessary for the development of intelligence and for the ultimate welfare, happiness, and usefulness of the child.

Even so is it with the difficulties of life with which older children are confronted, and which it is imperative, for their own growth and development, that they should solve and surmount. And each difficulty solved means so much more experience gained, so much more insight and wisdom acquired. It means a valuable lesson learned, with the added gladness and freedom of a task successfully accomplished.

Difficulties Are Necessary for Progress

What is the real nature of a difficulty? Is it not a situation which is not fully grasped and understood in all its bearings? As such, it calls for the development and exercise of a deeper insight and broader intelligence than has previously been exercised. It is an urgent necessity calling forth unused energy, and demanding the expression and employment of latent power and hidden resources. It is, therefore, a good angel, albeit disguised; a friend, a teacher; and, when calmly listened to and rightly understood, leads to larger blessedness and higher wisdom.

Without difficulties there could be no progress, no unfoldment, no evolution. Universal stagnation would prevail, and humanity would perish of boredom.

Let a man rejoice when he is confronted with obstacles, for it means that he has reached the end of some particular line of indifference or folly. He is now called upon to summon up all his energy and intelligence in order to extricate himself, and to find a better way. The powers within him are crying out for greater freedom, for enlarged exercise and scope.

No situation can be difficult of itself. It is the lack of insight into its intricacies, and the want of wisdom in dealing with it, which give rise to the difficulty.

Immeasurable, therefore, is the gain of a difficulty transcended.

Difficulties do not spring into existence arbitrarily and accidentally. They have their causes, and are called forth by the law of evolution itself, by the growing necessities of the man's being. Herein resides their blessedness.

Difficulties Are a Two-Way Street

There are ways of conduct which end inevitably in complications and perplexities, and there are ways of conduct which lead, just as inevitably, out of troublesome complexities. However tightly a man may have bound himself round, he can always unbind himself. Into whatever morasses of trouble and trackless wastes of bewilderment he may have ignorantly wandered, he can always find his way out again. He can always recover the lost highway of uninvolved simplicity which leads, straight and clear, to the sunny city of wise and blessed action.

But he will never do this by sitting down and weeping in despair, nor by complaining, worrying, and aimlessly wishing he were differently situated. His dilemma calls for alertness, logical thought, and calm calculation. His position requires that he shall strongly command himself; that he shall think and search, and rouse himself to strenuous and unremitting exertion in order to regain himself.

Worry and anxiety only serve to heighten the gloom and exaggerate the magnitude of the difficulty. If he will but quietly take himself to task, and retrace in thought, the more or less intricate way by which he has come to his present position, he will soon perceive where he made mistakes.

He will discover those places where he took a false turn, and where a little more thoughtfulness, judgement, economy, or self-denial would have saved him. He will see how, step by step, he has involved himself, and how a riper judgement and clearer wisdom would have enabled him to take an altogether different and truer course.

Having proceeded thus far, and extracted from his past conduct this priceless grain of golden wisdom, his difficulty will already have assumed less impregnable proportions. He will then be able to bring to bear upon it the searchlight of dispassionate thought, thoroughly analyze it, to comprehend it in all its details, and to perceive the relation which those details bear to the motive surrounding the action and conduct within himself. This being done, the difficulty will have ceased, for the straight way out of it will plainly appear, and the man will thus have learned, for all time, his lesson. He will have gained an item of wisdom and a measure of blessedness of which he can never again be deprived.

Difficulties Are Opportunities

Just as there are ways of ignorance, selfishness, folly, and blindness which end in confusion and perplexity, so there are ways of knowledge, self-denial, wisdom, and insight which lead to pleasant and peaceful conditions. He who knows this will meet difficulties in a courageous spirit, and, in overcoming them, will evolve truth out of error, bliss out of pain, and peace out of disturbance.

No man can be confronted with a difficulty which he has not the strength to meet and subdue. Worry is not merely useless, it is folly, for it defeats that power and intelligence which is otherwise equal to the task. Every difficulty can be overcome if rightly dealt with. Anxiety is, therefore, unnecessary. The task which cannot be overcome ceases to be a difficulty, and becomes an impossibility; and anxiety is still unnecessary, for there is only one way of dealing with an impossibility— namely, to submit to it. The inevitable is the best.

> *"Heartily know,*
> *When half-gods go,*
> *The gods arrive."*

And just as domestic, social, and economic difficulties are born of ignorance and lead to riper knowledge, so every religious doubt, every mental perplexity, every heart-beclouding shadow, foretells greater spiritual gain, and is prophetic of a brighter dawn of intelligence for him on whom it falls.

The Beginning of a New Day

It is a great day in the life of a man (though at the time he knows it not) when bewildering perplexities concerning the mystery of life take possession of his mind, for it signifies that his era of dead indifference, of animal sloth, of mere vegetative happiness, has come to an end. Henceforth he shall live as an aspiring, self-evolving being. No longer a mere human animal, he will now begin to live as a man. He will exert all his mental energies to the solution of life's problems, to the answering of those haunting perplexities which are the sentinels of truth, and which stand at the gate and threshold of the Temple of Wisdom.

> "He it is who, when great trials come,
> Nor seeks nor shuns them, but doth calmly stay."

Nor will he ever rest again in selfish ease and listless ignorance; nor sleekly satisfy himself with the swine's husks of fleshly pleasure. He will not find a hiding-place from the ceaseless whisperings of his heart's dark and indefinable questions. The divine within him has been awakened. A sleeping god is shaking off the incoherent visions of the night. Never again will he slumber, never again will he rest, until his eyes settle upon the full, broad day of Truth.

It is impossible for such a man to hush, for any length of time, the call to higher purposes and achievements which is aroused within him. For the awakened faculties of his being will ceaselessly urge him on to unravel his perplexities. For him, there shall be no more peace in sin, no more rest in error, no final refuge but in Wisdom.

Mastering Your Lessons

Great will be the blessedness of such a man when, conscious of the ignorance of which his doubts and perplexities are born, he acknowledges and understands that ignorance. And rather than striving to

The Wisdom of James Allen III ~

hide himself from from it, he earnestly applies himself to its removal. Then he will seek unremittingly, day after day, for that pathway of light which shall dispel all the dark shadows, dissolve his doubts, and find the solution to all his pressing problems.

And as a child is glad when he has mastered a lesson long toiled over, so a man's heart becomes light and free when he has satisfactorily met some worldly difficulty. Even so, but to a far greater degree, will a man's heart be rendered joyous and peaceful when some vital and eternal question, which has been long brooded over and grappled with, is at last completely answered, and its darkness is forever dispelled.

Do not regard your difficulties and perplexities as ominous signs of ill; by so doing you will make them ill. Regard them as prophetic of good, which, indeed, they are. Do not persuade yourself that you can evade them; you cannot. Do not try to run away from them. This is impossible, for wherever you go they will still be there with you. Meet them calmly and bravely. Confront them with all the dispassion and dignity which you can command. Weigh up their proportions. Analyze them; grasp their details; measure their strength; understand them; attack them, and finally vanquish them.

~ Byways of Blessedness

Thus will you develop strength and intelligence. Thus will you enter one of those byways of blessedness which are hidden from the superficial gaze.

*"Man who would be
Must rule the empire of himself; in it
Must be supreme, establishing his throne
On vanquished will, quelling the anarchy
Of hopes and fears, being himself alone."*
—Shelley

*"Have you missed in your aim? Well, the mark is still shining.
Did you faint in the race? Well, take breath for the next."*
—Ella Wheeler Wilcox

Burden-Dropping

WE HEAR AND READ much about burden-bearing, but of the better way of burden-dropping very little is heard or known. Yet why should you go about with an oppressive weight at your heart when you might relieve yourself of it and move amongst your fellows heart-free and cheerful?

No man carries a load upon his back necessarily except to transfer something from one place to another. He does not saddle his shoulders with a perpetual burden, and then regard himself as a martyr for his pains. So why should you impose upon your mind a useless burden, and then add to its weight the miseries of self-condolence and self-pity? Why not abandon both your load and your misery, and thus add to the happiness of the world by first making yourself happy? No reason can justify, and no logic support, the ceaseless carrying of a grievous load.

As in things material, a load is only undertaken as

a necessary means of transference, and is never a source of sorrow. So in things spiritual a burden should only be taken up as a means towards some good and necessary end, which, when attained, the burden is put aside. Then, the carrying of such a burden, far from being a source of grief, would be a cause for rejoicing.

We say that bodily mortifications which some religious ascetics inflict upon themselves are unnecessary and vain. Yet are the mental mortifications, which so many people inflict upon themselves, less unnecessary and vain?

All Burdens Are of The Mind
Where is the burden which should cause unhappiness or sorrow? It does not exist. If a thing is to be done let it be done cheerfully, and not with inward groanings and lamentations. It is of the highest wisdom to embrace necessity as a friend and guide. It is of the greatest folly to scowl upon necessity as an enemy, and to wish or try to overcome or avoid it. We meet our own at every turn, and duties only become oppressive loads when we refuse to recognize and embrace them.

He who does any necessary thing in a begrudging and complaining spirit, while hunting after unnecessary pleasures, lashes himself with the scorpions of misery and disappointment. He imposes upon himself a doubly-weighted burden of weariness and unrest under which he incessantly groans.

> *"Wake thou, O self, to better things;*
> *To yonder heights uplift thy wings;*
> *Take up the psalm of life anew;*
> *Sing of the good, sing of the true;*
> *Sing of full victory o'er wrong;*
> *Make thou a richer, sweeter song;*
> *Out of thy doubting, care and pain*
> *Weave thou a joyous, glad refrain;*
> *Out of thy thorns a crown weave thou*
> *Of rare rejoicing. Sing thou, now."*

I will give my cheerful, unselfish, and undivided attention to the doing of all those things which enter into my pact with life. And though I walk under colossal responsibilities, I shall be unconscious of any troublesome weight or grievous burden.

You say a certain thing (a duty, a companionship, or a social obligation) troubles you, is burdensome, and you resign yourself to oppression with the thought: "I have entered into this, and will go through with it, but it is a heavy and grievous work."

But is the thing really burdensome, or is it your selfishness that is oppressing you? I tell you that that very thing which you regard as so imprisoning a restriction is the first gateway to your emancipation. That work which you regard as a perpetual curse contains for you the actual blessedness which you vainly persuade yourself lies in another and unapproachable direction.

Reflections of The Inner Self

All things are mirrors in which you see yourself reflected, and the gloom which you perceive in your work is but a reflection of that mental state which you bring to it. Bring a right, unselfish, state of heart to the thing, and lo! it is at once transformed. It becomes a means of strength and blessedness, reflecting back that which you have brought to it. If you bring a scowling face to your looking glass will you complain of the glass that it glowers upon you with a deformed visage, or will you put your face right, and so get back from the mirror a more pleasing countenance?

If it is right and necessary that a thing should be done then the doing of it is good, and it can only become burdensome in wishing not to do it. The selfish wish makes the thing appear evil. If it is neither right nor necessary that a thing should be done then the doing of it in order to gain some coveted pleasure is folly, which can only lead to burdensome issues.

The duty which you shirk is your reproving angel; the pleasure which you race after is your flattering enemy. Foolish man! when will you turn round and be wise?

You Create Your Own Suffering

It is the beneficence of the universe that is everywhere, and at all times, urging its creatures to wisdom just as it demands coherence of its atoms. That folly and selfishness entail suffering in ever-increasing degrees of intensity is preservative and good. For agony is the enemy of apathy and the herald of wisdom.

What is painful? What is grievous? What is burdensome? Passion is painful. Folly is serious. Selfishness is burdensome.

> *"It is the dark idolatry of self*
> *Which, when our thoughts and actions*
>   *once are done,*
> *Demands that man should weep,*
>   *and bleed, and groan."*

Eliminate passion, folly, and selfishness from your

mind and conduct and you will eliminate suffering from your life. Burden-dropping consists in abandoning the inward selfishness and putting pure love in its place. Go to your task with love in your heart and you will go to it light-hearted and cheerful.

The mind, through ignorance creates its own burdens and inflicts its own punishments. No one is doomed to carry any load. Sorrow is not arbitrarily imposed. These things are self-made. Reason is the rightful monarch of the mind, and anarchy reigns when the throne is usurped by passion. When love of pleasure is to the fore, heaviness and anguish compose the rear. You are free to choose.

Even if you are bound by passion, and feel helpless, you have bound yourself, and are not helpless. Where you have bound you can unbind. You have come to your present state by degrees, and you can recover yourself by degrees. You can reinstate reason and dethrone passion. The time to avoid evil is before pleasure is embraced, but, once embraced, its train of consequences should teach you wisdom. The time to decide is before responsibilities are adopted, but, once adopted, all selfish considerations, with their attendant grumblings, whinings, and complaining, should be religiously excluded from the heart. Responsibilities lose their weight when carried lovingly and wisely.

Selfishness Increases Suffering

What heavy burden is a man weighted with which is not made heavier and more unendurable by weak thoughts of selfish desires? If your circumstances are "trying" it is because you need them and can evolve the strength to meet them. They are trying because there is some weak spot within you, and they will continue to be trying until that spot is eradicated. Be glad that you have the opportunity of becoming stronger and wiser. No circumstances can be trying to wisdom; nothing can weary love. Stop brooding over your own trying circumstances and contemplate the lives of some of those about you.

Parable of Two Women

Here is a woman with a large family who has to make ends meet on a meager wage. She performs all her domestic duties, down to the washing. She finds time to attend sick neighbors, and manages to keep entirely out of the two common quagmires—debt and despondency. She is cheerful from morning to night, and never complains of her "trying circumstances." She is perennially cheerful because she is unselfish.

She is happy in the thought that she is the means of happiness to others.

Were she to brood upon the holidays, the pretty baubles, the lazy hours of which she is deprived; of the plays she cannot see, the music she cannot hear, the books she cannot read, the parties she cannot attend, the good she might do, the friendships she is debarred from forming; of the many pleasures which might only be hers if her circumstances were more favorable—if she brooded thus what a miserable creature she would be!

How unbearably laborious her work would become! How every little domestic duty would hang like a millstone about her neck, dragging her down to the grave which, unless she altered her state of mind, she would quickly reach, killed by—selfishness! But, not living in vain desires for herself, she is relieved of all burdens, and is happy. Cheerfulness and unselfishness are sworn friends. Love knows no heavy toil.

Here is another woman, with a private income which is more than sufficient, combined with leisure and luxury. Yet, because she is called upon to forfeit a portion of her time, pleasure, and money to discharge some obligation which she wishes to be rid of, and which should be to her a work of loving service, she is perpetually discontented and unhappy. Fostering in her heart some ungratified desire, she complains of "trying circumstances." Discontent and selfishness are inseparable companions. Self-love knows no joyful labor.

Of the two sets of circumstances depicted above (and life is crowded with such contrasted instances) which are the "trying" conditions? Is it not true that neither of them are trying, and that both are blest or unblest in accordance with the measure of love or selfishness which is infused into them? Is not the root of the whole matter in the mind of the individual and not in the circumstance?

Love Is Manifested Here and Now

When a man, who has recently taken up the study of some branch of theology, religion, or "occultism," says: "If I had not burdened myself with a wife and family I could have done a great work. And had I known years ago what I know now, I would never have married." I know that man has not yet found the commonest and broadest way of wisdom (for there is no greater folly than regret), and that he is incapable of the great work which he is so ambitious to perform.

If a man has such deep love for his fellow-men

that he is anxious to do a great work for humanity, he will manifest that surpassing love always and in the place where he now is. His home will be filled with it, and the beauty, sweetness, and peace of his unselfish love will follow wherever he goes, making happy those about him and transmuting all things into good. The love that goes abroad to air itself, and is undiscoverable at home, is not love—it is vanity.

Have I not seen (Oh, pitiful sight!) the cheerless home and neglected children of the misguided missionary and religionist? It is on such self-delusion as this that self-pity and self-martyrdom ever wait. Its self-inflicted misery is regarded by the deluded one as a holy and religious burden which he or she is called upon to bear.

Only a great man can do a great work; and he will be great wherever he is, and will do his noble work under whatsoever conditions he may find himself when he has unfolded and revealed that work.

You who are so anxious to work for humanity, to help your fellow men, begin that work at home. Help yourself, your neighbor, your wife, your child. Do not be deluded. Until you do, with utmost faithfulness, the nearer and the lesser, you cannot do the farther and greater.

The Wisdom of James Allen III ~

Waking Up to The Truth!

If a man has lived many years of his life in lust and selfish pleasure, it is in the order of things that his accumulated errors should at last weigh heavily upon him. For until they are thus brought home to him, he will not abandon them. He will not exert himself to find a better life. But while he regards his self-made, self-imposed burdens as "holy crosses" imposed upon him by the Supreme, or as marks of superior virtue, or as loads which fate, circumstances, or other people have heaped undeservedly and unjustly upon him, he is but lengthening out his folly. He is increasing the weight of his burdens, and multiplying pain and sorrow.

Only when such a man wakes up to the truth that his burdens are of his own making, that they are the accumulated effects of his own acts, will he cease from self-pity and find the better way of burden-dropping. Only when he opens his eyes to see that his every thought and act is another brick, another stone, built into the temple of life will he develop the insight which will enable him to recognize his own unstable handiwork, the unflinching manliness to acknowledge it, and the courage to build more nobly and enduringly.

Painful burdens are necessary, but only so long as we lack love and wisdom.

~ Byways of Blessedness

The Temple of Blessedness lies beyond the outer courts of suffering and humiliation and to reach it the pilgrim must pass through the outer courts. For a time he will linger in the outer, but only so long as, through his own imperfect understanding, he mistakes it for the inner. While he pities himself and confounds suffering with holiness, he will remain in suffering. But when, casting off the last unholy rag of self-pity, he perceives that suffering is a means and not an end, and that despair is a state self-originated and self-propagated. Then, converted and right-minded, he will rapidly pass through the outer courts, and reach the inner abode of peace.

Suffering Slowly Accumulates

Suffering does not originate in the perfect but in the imperfect. It does not mark the complete but the incomplete. It can, therefore, be transcended. Its self-born cause can be found, investigated, comprehended, and forever removed.

It is true therefore, that we must pass through agony to rest, through loneliness to peace. But let the sufferer not forget that it is a "passing through;" that the agony is a gateway and not a habitation; that the loneliness is a pathway and not a destination; and that a little farther on, he will come to painless and blissful repose.

Little by little a burden is accumulated; imperceptibly and by degrees its weight is increased. A thoughtless impulse, a gross self-indulgence, a blind passion yielded to and gratified again and again; an impure thought fostered, a cruel word uttered, a foolish thing done time after time, and at last the gathered weight of many follies becomes oppressive.

At first, and for a time, the weight is not felt. But it is being added to day after day, and the time comes when the accumulated burden is felt in all its galling weight. The bitter fruits of error are gathered, and the heart is troubled with the weariness of life. When this period arrives let the sufferer look to himself. Let him search for the blessed way of burden-dropping. Once found, he will find wisdom to live better, purity to live sweeter, love to live nobler. He will find, in the reversal of that conduct by which these burdens were accumulated, light-hearted nights and days, cheerful action, and unclouded joy.

"Come out of the world—come above it—
Up over its crosses and graves;
Though the green earth is fair and I love it,
We must love it as masters, not slaves,

~ Byways of Blessedness

*Come up where the dust never rises—
But only the perfume of flowers—
And life shall be glad with surprises
Of beautiful hours."*

*"This to me is life;
That if life be a burden, I will join
To make it but the burden of a song."*
—Bailey

*"Have you heard that it was good to gain the day?
I also say it is good to fall, battles are lost in the
same spirit in which they are won."*
—Walt Whitman

Hidden Sacrifices

IT IS ONE OF THE PARADOXES of Truth that we gain by giving up; we lose by greedily grasping. Every gain in virtue necessitates some loss in vice; every accession of holiness means some selfish pleasure yielded up; and every forward step on the path of Truth demands the forfeit of some self-assertive error.

He who would be clothed in new garments must first cast away the old, and he who would find the True must sacrifice the false. The gardener digs in the weeds in order that they may feed, with their decay, the plants which are good for food; and the Tree of Wisdom can only flourish on the compost of uprooted follies. Growth—gain—necessitates sacrifice—loss.

The true life, the blessed life, the life that is not tormented with passions and pains, is reached only through sacrifice, not necessarily the sacrifice of outward things, but the sacrifice of the inward errors and defilements, for it is these, and these only, which bring misery into life. It is not the good and true that needs to be sacrificed but the evil and false. Therefore all sacrifice is ultimately gain, and there is no essential loss. Yet at first the loss seems great, and the sacrifice is painful, but this is because of the self-delusion and spiritual blindness which always accompany selfishness, and pain must always accompany the cutting away of some selfish portion of one's nature.

Sacrifice Is Eventual Gain

When the drunkard resolves to sacrifice his lust for strong drink he passes through a period of great suffering, and he feels that he is forfeiting a great pleasure. But when his victory is complete, when the lust is dead, and his mind is calm and sober, then he knows that he has gained incalculably by the giving up of his selfish animal pleasure. What he has lost was evil and false and not worth keeping—nay, its keeping entailed continual misery—but what he has gained in character, in self-control, in soberness and greater peace of mind, is good and true, and it was necessary that he should acquire it.

So it is with all true sacrifice. It is at first, and until it is completed, painful, and this is why men shrink from it. They cannot see any purpose in abstaining from and overcoming selfish gratification. It seems to them like losing so much that is sweet; seems to them like courting misery, and giving up all happiness and pleasure. And this must be so. For if a man could know that by giving up his particular forms of selfishness his gain in happiness would be immeasurably greater, unselfishness (which is now so difficult to attain) would then be rendered infinitely more difficult to achieve. For his desire for the greater gain—his selfishness—would thereby be greatly intensified.

No man can become unselfish, and thereby arrive at the highest bliss, until he is willing to lose, looking for neither gain nor reward. It is this state of mind which constitutes unselfishness. A man must be willing to humbly sacrifice his selfish habits and practices because they are untrue and unworthy, and for the happiness of those about him, without expecting any reward or looking for any good to accrue to himself. Nay, he must be prepared to lose for himself, to forfeit pleasure and happiness, even life itself, if by so doing he can make the world more beautiful and happy.

But does he really lose? Does the miser lose when he gives up his lust for gold? Does the thief lose when he abandons stealing? Does the libertine lose when he sacrifices his unworthy pleasures? No man loses by the sacrifice of self, or some portion of self. Nevertheless, he thinks he will lose by so doing, and because he so thinks, he suffers, and this is where the sacrifice comes in—this is where he gains by losing.

Hidden Sacrifices of The Heart

All true sacrifice is within. It is spiritual and hidden, and is prompted by deep humility of heart. Nothing but the sacrifice of self can avail, and to this all men must come sooner or later during their spiritual evolution. But in what does this self-surrender consist? How is it practiced? Where is it sought and found? It consists in overcoming the daily proneness to selfish thoughts and acts. It is practiced in our common interaction with others. And it is found in the hour of tumult and temptation.

There are hidden sacrifices of the heart which are infinitely blessed both to those who make them and those for whom they are made, even though their making costs much effort and some pain. Men are anxious to do some great thing, to perform some great sacrifice which lies beyond the realm of their experience, while all the time, perhaps, they are neglecting the one thing needful. They are blind to that sacrifice which by its very nearness is rendered imperative.

Where lurks your obsessive sin? Where lies your weakness? Where does temptation assail you most strongly? There shall you make your first sacrifice, and shall find thereby the way unto your peace.

Perhaps it is anger or unkindness. Are you prepared to sacrifice the angry impulse and word, the unkind thought and deed? Are you prepared to silently endure abuse, attack, accusation, and unkindness, refusing to pay back these in their own coin? Moreover, are you prepared to give in return for these dark follies kindness and loving protection? If so, then you are ready to make those hidden sacrifices which lead to blessed bliss.

Sacrificing Anger and Unkindness

If you are given to anger or unkindness, offer it up. These hard, cruel, and wrong conditions of mind never brought you any good. They can never bring you anything but unrest, misery, and spiritual blindness. Nor can they ever bring to others anything but unhappiness.

Perhaps you will say: "But he was unkind to me

first; he treated me unjustly." Perhaps so, but what a poor excuse is this! What an unmanly and ineffectual refuge! For if his unkindness toward you is so wrong and hurtful, yours to him must be equally so. Because another is unkind to you is no justification of your own unkindness, but is rather a call for the exercise of greater kindness on your part. Can the pouring in of more water prevent a flood? Neither can unkindness lessen unkindness. Can fire quench fire? Neither can anger overcome anger.

Offer up all unkindness, all anger. "It takes two to make a quarrel;" don't be the "other one." If one is angry or unkind to you try to find out where you have acted wrongly; and, whether you have acted wrongly or not, do not throw back the angry word or unkind act. Remain silent, self-contained, and kindly disposed. Learn, by continual effort in right-doing, to have compassion upon the wrong-doer.

Sacrificing Impatience and Irritability

Perhaps you are habitually impatient and irritable. Know, then, the hidden sacrifice which it is needful that you should make. Give up your impatience. Overcome it there where it will not assert itself. Resolve that you will yield no longer to its tyrannical

The Wisdom of James Allen III ~

sway but will conquer it and cast it out. It is not worth keeping a single hour, nor would it dominate you for another moment if you were not laboring under the delusion that the follies and perversities of others render impatience on your part necessary.

Whatever others may do or say, even though they may mock and taunt you, impatience is not only unnecessary, it can never do anything other than aggravate the evil which it seeks to remove. Calm, strong, and deliberate action can accomplish much, but impatience and its accompanying irritability are always indications of weakness and inefficiency. And what do they bestow upon you? Do they bestow rest, peace, happiness, or bring these to those about you? Do they not, rather, make you and those about you wretched? But though your impatience may hurt others it certainly hurts, wounds, and impoverishes yourself most of all.

Nor can the impatient man know anything of true blessedness, for he is a continual source of trouble and unrest to himself. The calm beauty and perpetual sweetness of patience are unknown to him, and peace cannot draw near to soothe and comfort him.

There is no blessedness anywhere until impatience is sacrificed. Its sacrifice means the development of endurance, the practice of forbearance, and the creation of a new and gentler habit of mind. When impatience and irritability are entirely put away, are finally offered up on the altar of unselfishness, then is the blessedness of a strong, quiet, and peaceful mind realized and enjoyed.

> *"Each hour we think*
> *Of others more than self, that hour we live again,*
> *And every lowly sacrifice we make*
> *For others' good shall make life more than self,*
> *And open the windows of thy soul to light*
> *From higher spheres. So hail thy lot with joy."*

Sacrificing Little Indulgences

Then there are little selfish indulgences, some of which appear harmless, and are commonly fostered. But no selfish indulgence can be harmless, and men and women do not know what they lose by repeatedly and habitually succumbing to selfish gratifications. If the God in man is to rise strong and triumphant, the beast in man must perish.

The pandering to the animal nature, even when it appears innocent and seems sweet, leads away from truth and blessedness. Each time you give way to the animal nature within you, and feed and gratify it, that nature waxes stronger and more rebellious, and takes firmer possession of your mind, which should be in the keeping of Truth.

Not until a man has sacrificed some apparently trivial indulgence does he discover what strength, what joy, what poise of character and holy influence he has all along been losing by that gratification. Not until a man sacrifices his hankering for pleasure does he enter into the fullness of abiding joy.

By his personal indulgences a man demeans himself, forfeits self-respect to the extent and frequency of his indulgence, and deprives himself of exemplary influence and the power to accomplish lasting good in his work in the world. He also, by allowing himself to be led by blind desire, increases his mental blindness, and fails of that ultimate clearness of vision, that clarified perception which pierces to the heart of things and comprehends the real and the true.

Animal indulgence is alien to the perception of Truth. By the sacrifice of his indulgences man rises above confusion and doubt, and arrives at the possession of insight and surety.

Sacrifice your cherished and coveted indulgence. Fix your mind on something higher, nobler, and more enduring than ephemeral pleasure. Live superior to the craving for sense-excitement, and you will live neither vainly nor uncertainly.

Sacrifice of Self-Assertion

A practice which is very far-reaching in its effect upon others, and rich with the revelations of Truth for him who makes it, is the sacrifice of self-assertion. This is the giving up of all interference with the lives, views, or religion of other people, substituting for it an understanding love and sympathy.

Self-assertion or opinionativeness is a form of egotism or selfishness most generally found in connection with intellectualism and dialectical skill. It is blindly presumptive and uncharitable, and, more often than not, is regarded as a virtue. But when once the mind has opened to perceive the way of gentleness and self-sacrificing love, then the ignorance, deformity, and painful nature of self-assertion become apparent.

The victim of self-assertion sets up his own opinion as the standard of right and the measure of judgement. He regards all those as wrong whose lives and opinions run counter to his own. And, being eager to put others right, is thereby prevented from putting himself right. His attitude of mind brings about opposition and contradiction from people who are anxious to put him right. This wounds his vanity and makes him miserable, so that he lives in an almost continual fever of unhappy, resentful and uncharitable thoughts.

There can be no peace for such a man, no true knowledge, and no advancement until he sacrifices his desire to bend others to his own way of thinking and acting. Nor can he understand the hearts of others, and enter lovingly into their strivings and aspirations. His mind is cramped and embittered, and he is shut out from all sweet sympathy and spiritual communion.

He who sacrifices the spirit of self-assertion, who in his daily contact with others puts aside his prejudices and opinions, and strives both to learn from others and to understand them as they are, who allows to others perfect liberty (such as he exercises himself) to form their own opinions, their own way in life—such a man will acquire a deeper insight, a broader charity, and a richer bliss than he has previously experienced. He will strike a byway of blessedness from which he was formerly shut out.

Sacrifice of Greed

Then there is the sacrifice of greed and all greedy thoughts. The willingness that others should possess rather than we; the not-coveting of things for ourselves but rejoicing that they are possessed and enjoyed by others and that they bring happiness to others; the ceasing to claim one's "own," and the giving up to others, unselfishly and without malice, that which they require as payment. This attitude of mind is a source of deep peace and great spiritual strength. It is the sacrifice of self-interest.

Material possessions are temporary, and in this sense we cannot truly call them our own—they are merely in our keeping for a short time. But spiritual possessions are eternal and must ever remain with us. Unselfishness is a spiritual possession which is only secured by ceasing to covet material possessions and enjoyments, by ceasing to regard things as for our own special and exclusive pleasure, and by our readiness to yield them up for the good of others.

The unselfish man, even though he finds himself involved in riches, stands aloof, in his mind, from the idea of "exclusive possession." And so he escapes the bitterness, fear, and anxiety which ever accompany the covetous spirit. He does not regard any of his outward accumulations as being too valuable to lose, but he regards the virtue of unselfishness as being too valuable to the world—to suffering humanity—to lose or cast away. He is ever ready to give up what he has for the good and happiness of others

And who is the blessed man? He who is ever hankering after more possessions, thinking only of the personal pleasure he can get out of them? Or he who is ever ready to give up what he has for the good and happiness of others? By greed happiness is destroyed; by not-greed happiness is restored.

Sacrificing Bitter Thoughts

Another hidden sacrifice, one of great spiritual beauty and of powerful efficacy in the healing of human sorrows, is the sacrifice of hatred—the giving up of all bitter thoughts against others, of all malice, dislike, and resentment. Bitter thoughts and blessedness cannot dwell together. Hatred is a fierce fire that scorches up all the sweet flowers of peace and happiness in the heart of him who harbors it. It makes a hell of every place where it comes.

Hatred has many names and many forms but only one essence—namely, burning thoughts of resentment against others. It is sometimes called by the name of religion, by its blind, zealous devotees, causing them to attack, slander, and persecute each other because they will not accept each other's views of life and death, thus filling the earth with miseries and tears.

All resentment, dislike, ill-thinking, and ill-speaking of others is hatred, and where there is hatred there is always unhappiness. No one has conquered hatred while thoughts of resentment towards others spring up in his mind. This sacrifice is not complete until a man can think kindly of those who try to do him wrong. Yet it must be made before true blessedness can be realized and known. Beyond the hard, cruel, steely gates of hatred waits the divine angel of love, ready to reveal herself to anyone who will subdue and sacrifice hateful thoughts, and conduct him to his peace.

Whatever others may say of you, whatever they may do to you, never take offense. Do not return hatred with hatred. If another hates you perhaps you have, consciously or unconsciously, failed somewhere in your conduct. Or there may be some misunderstanding which the exercise of a little gentleness and reason may remove. But, under all circumstances, "Father, forgive them" is infinitely better, sweeter, and nobler than "I will have nothing more to do with them." Hatred is so small and poor, so blind and wretched. Love is so great and rich, so far-seeing and blissful.

"The highest culture is to speak no ill:
The best reformer is the man whose eyes

> *Are quick to see all beauty and all worth;*
> *And by his own discreet, well-ordered life*
> *Alone reproves the erring."*

Sacrifice all hatred, slay it upon the holy altar of devotion—devotion to others. Think no more of any injury to your own petty self, but see to it that henceforth you injure and wound no other. Open the flood gates of your heart for the inpouring of that sweet, great, beautiful love which embraces all with strong yet tender thoughts of protection and peace, leaving no one, nay, not even he who hates, despises, or slanders you, out in the cold.

Sacrificing Other Impurities

Then there is the hidden sacrifice of impure desires, of weak self-pity and degrading self-praise, of vanity and pride, for these are unblest attitudes of mind and deformities of heart. He who makes them, one by one, gradually subduing and overcoming them, will, according to the measure of his success, rise above weakness, suffering, and sorrow. He will comprehend and enjoy perfect and imperishable blessedness.

Now, all these hidden sacrifices which are here mentioned are pure, humble heart-offerings. They are made within; are offered up on the sacred, lonely, unseen altar of one's own heart. Not one of them can be made until the fault is first silently acknowledged and confessed. No man can sacrifice an error until he first of all confesses to himself, "I am in error." When yielding it up, he will perceive and receive the truth which his error formerly obscured.

The Final Refuge of Sacrifice

"The kingdom of heaven cometh not by observation." The silent sacrifice of self for the good of others, the daily giving up of one's egotistic tendencies, this is not seen and rewarded by the public. It brings no loud display of popularity and praise. It is hidden away from the eyes of all the world, nay, even from the gaze of those who are nearest to you, for no eyes of flesh can perceive its spiritual beauty. But think not that because it is unperceived it is therefore futile. Its blissful radiance is enjoyed by you, and its power for good over others is great and far-reaching. For though others cannot see it, nor, perhaps understand it, they are yet unconsciously influenced by it.

They will not know what silent battles you are fighting, what eternal victories over self you are achieving. But, they will feel your altered attitude, your new mind, wrought of the fabric of love and loving thoughts, and they will share somewhat in its happiness and bliss. They will know nothing of the frequent fierceness of the fight you are waging, of the wounds you receive and the healing balm you apply, of the anguish and the after-peace. But they will know that you have grown sweeter and gentler, stronger and more silently self-reliant, more patient and pure, and that they are rested and helped by your presence.

What rewards can compare with this? Beside the fragrant duties of love the praises of men are gross and offensive, and in the pure flame of a selfless heart the flatteries of the world are turned to ashes. Love is its own reward, its own joy, its own satisfaction. It is the final refuge and resting-place of passion-tortured souls.

Look Within for The Light

The sacrifice of self, and the acquisition of the supreme knowledge and bliss which it confers, is not accomplished by one great and glorious act. Rather it is achieved by a series of lesser and successive sacrifices in the ordinary life of the world, by a succession of steps in the daily conquest of Truth over selfishness. He who each day accomplishes some victory over himself, who subdues and puts behind him some unkind thought, some impure desire, some tendency to sin, is everyday growing stronger, purer, and wiser. Every dawn finds him nearer to that final glory of Truth which each self-sacrificing act reveals in part.

Look not outside you nor beyond you for the light and blessedness of Truth, but look within. You will find it within the narrow sphere of your duty, even in the humble and hidden sacrifices of your own heart.

"What need hath man
 Of Eden passed, or Paradise to come,
 When heaven is round us and within ourselves?

"Lowliness is the base of every virtue:
 Who goes the lowest, builds doubt not, the safest."
—*Bailey*

"Truth is within ourselves; it takes noise
 From outward things, whate'er you may believe."
—*Browning*

Sympathy

WE CAN ONLY SYMPATHIZE with others in so far as we have conquered ourselves. We cannot think and feel for others while we are engaged in condoling with and pitying ourselves. We cannot deal tenderly and lovingly with others while we are anxious for our own pre-eminence or for the exclusive preservation of ourselves, our opinions, and our own, generally. What is sympathy but thoughtfulness for others in the forgetfulness of self?

To Sympathize with others we must first understand them. And to understand them we must put away all personal preconceptions concerning them, and must see them as they are. We must enter into their inner state and become one with them, looking through their mental eyes and comprehending the range of their experience.

You cannot, of course, do this with a being whose wisdom and experience are greater than your own. Nor can you do it with any if you regard yourself as being on a higher plane than others (for egotism and sympathy cannot dwell together). But you can practice it with all those who are involved in sins and sufferings from which you have successfully extricated yourself. And, though your sympathy cannot embrace and overshadow the man whose greatness is beyond you, you can yet place yourself in such an attitude towards him as to receive the protection of his larger sympathy. Thus you make for yourself an easier way out of the sins and sufferings by which you are still enchained.

Barriers to Sympathy

Prejudice and ill-will are complete barriers to the giving of sympathy, while pride and vanity are total barriers to its reception. You cannot sympathize with a person for whom you have conceived a hatred. You cannot enjoy the sympathy of one whom you envy. You cannot understand the person whom you dislike, or him for whom, through animal impulse, you have framed an ill-formed affection. You do not, cannot, see him as he is, but see only your own imperfect notions of him. You see only a distorted image of him through the exaggerating medium of your ill-grounded opinions.

To see others as they are you must not allow impulsive likes or dislikes, powerful prejudices, or egotistic considerations to come between you and them. You must not resent their actions or condemn their beliefs and opinions. You must leave yourself entirely out, and must, for the time being, assume their position. Only in this way can you become *en rapport* with them, and so fathom their life, their experience, and understand it. For when a man is understood it becomes impossible to condemn him.

Men misjudge, condemn, and avoid each other because they do not understand each other. And they do not understand each other because they have not overcome and purified ourselves.

No Difference Between Sinner and Saint

Life is growth, development, and evolution, and there is no essential distinction between the sinner and the saint. There is only a difference in degree. The saint was once a sinner. The sinner will one day be a saint. The sinner is the child. The saint is the grown man. He who separates himself from sinners, regarding them as wicked men to be avoided, is like a man avoiding contact with little children because they are unwise, disobedient, and play with toys.

All life is one, but it has a variety of manifestations. The flower bloom is not something distinct from the tree: it is a part of it. It is only another form of leaf. Steam is not something apart from water: it is but another form of water. And in like manner good is transmuted evil: the saint is the sinner developed and transformed.

The sinner is one whose understanding is undeveloped, and he ignorantly chooses wrong modes of action. The saint is one whose understanding is ripened, and wisely chooses right modes of action. The sinner condemns the sinner, condemnation being a wrong mode of action. The saint never condemns the sinner, remembering that he himself formerly occupied the same place, but thinks of him with deep sympathy. He regards him in the light of a younger brother or sister or friend, for sympathy is a right and enlightened mode of action.

The perfected saint, who gives sympathy to all, needs it of none, for he has transcended sin and suffering, and lives in the enjoyment of lasting bliss.

But all who suffer need sympathy, and all who sin must suffer. When a man comes to understand that every sin, whether of thought or deed, receives its just quota of suffering, he ceases to condemn and begins to sympathize. He sees the sufferings which sin entails; and he comes to such understanding by purifying himself.

Extending Sympathy to All

As a man purges himself of passions, as he transmutes his selfish desire and puts under foot his egotistic tendencies, he sounds the depths of all human experiences—all sins, sufferings, and sorrows, all motives, thoughts, and deeds—and he comprehends the moral law in its perfection.

Complete self-conquest is perfect knowledge and perfect sympathy. He who views others with the stainless vision of a pure heart views them with a pitying heart. He sees them as a part of himself, not as something defiled, separate, and distinct, but as his very self, sinning as he has sinned, suffering as he has suffered, sorrowing as he has sorrowed. Yet, nevertheless, he is glad in the knowledge that they will come, as he has come, to perfect peace at last.

The truly good and wise man cannot be a passionate partisan, but extends his sympathy to all. He sees no evil in others to be condemned and resisted. But he sees the sin which is pleasant to the sinner, and the after-sorrow and pain which the sinner does not see, and, when it overtakes him, does not understand.

A man's sympathy extends just so far as his wisdom reaches, and no further. A man only grows wiser as he grows more tender and compassionate. To narrow one's sympathy is to narrow one's heart, and so to darken and embitter one's life. To extend and broaden one's sympathy is to enlighten and gladden one's life, and to make plainer to others the way of light and gladness.

To sympathize with another is to receive his being into our own, to become one with him, for unselfish love indissolubly unites. He whose sympathy reaches out to and embraces all humankind and all living creatures has realized his identity and oneness with all. He comprehends the universal Love, Law, and Wisdom.

Understanding Sympathy

Man is shut out from Heaven, Peace, and Truth only in so far as he shuts out others from his sympathy. Where his compassion ends his darkness, torment, and turmoil begin. For to shut others out from our love is to shut ourselves out from the blessedness of love, and to become cramped in the dark prison of self.

> *"Whoever walks a furlong without sympathy walks to his own funeral dressed in a shroud."*

Only when one's sympathy is unlimited is the Eternal Light of Truth revealed; only in the Love that knows no restrictions is boundless bliss enjoyed.

Sympathy is bliss; in it is revealed the highest, purest blessedness. It is divine, for in its reciprocal light all thought of self is lost, and there remains only the pure joy of oneness with others, the inexpressible communion of spiritual identity. Where a man ceases to sympathize he ceases to live, ceases to see, to realize, and know.

One cannot truly be compassionate with others until all selfish considerations concerning them are put away. He who does this, and strives to see others as they are, strives to realize their particular sins, temptations, and sorrows, their beliefs, opinions, and prejudices. He comes at last to see exactly where they stand in their spiritual evolution, comprehending the radius of their experience. He knows that they cannot for the present act otherwise than they do.

He sees that their thoughts and acts are prompted by the extent of their knowledge, or their lack of knowledge, and that if they act blindly and foolishly it is because their knowledge and experience are immature, and they can only come to act more wisely by gradual growth into more enlightened states of mind.

He also sees that though this growth can be encouraged, helped, and stimulated by the influence of a riper example, by reasonable words and well-timed instruction, it cannot be unnaturally forced. The flowers of love and wisdom must have time to grow. The barren branches of hatred and folly cannot be pruned away all at once.

The Sin of One Is The Sin of All

A compassionate man finds the doorway into the inner world of those with whom he comes in contact. He opens it, enters in, and dwells with them in the hidden and sacred sanctuary of their being. And he finds nothing to hate, nothing to revile, nothing to condemn in that sacred place, but something to love and tend, and, in his own heart, room only for greater compassion, greater patience, and greater love.

He sees that he is one with them, that they are but another aspect of himself, that their natures are not different from his own, except in modification and degree, but are identical with it. If they are acting out certain sinful tendencies, he has only to look within to find the same tendencies in himself, although, perhaps, restrained or purified. If they are manifesting certain holy and divine qualities he finds the same pure spirit within himself, though, perhaps, in a lesser degree of power and development.

"One touch of nature makes the whole world kin."

The sin of one is the sin of all. The virtue of one is the virtue of all. Nobody can be separate from another. There is no difference of nature but only difference of condition. If a man thinks he is separated from another by virtue of his superior holiness, he is not so separated, and his darkness and delusion are very great. Humanity is one, and in the holy sanctuary of compassion saint and sinner meet and unite.

The Compassion of Jesus

It is said of Jesus that He took upon Himself the sins of the whole world—that is, He identified Himself with those sins, and did not regard Himself as essentially separate from sinners but as being of a like nature with them. This realization of His oneness with all men was manifested in His life as profound sympathy with those who, for their deep sins, were avoided and cast off by others.

And who is it that is in the greatest need of compassion? Not the saint, not the enlightened seer, not the perfect man. It is the sinner, the unenlightened man, the imperfect one; and the greater the sin the greater is the need. "I came not to call the righteous but sinners to repentance" is the statement of One who comprehended all human needs. The righteous do not need your sympathy. But the unrighteous man, he who, by his wrong-doing, is laying up long periods of suffering and woe is in need of it.

The Transformational Power of Sympathy

The flagrantly unrighteous man is condemned, despised, and avoided by those who are living in a similar condition to him, though for the time being, they may not be subject to his particular form of sin. That withholding of sympathy and that mutual condemnation which are so widespread is the commonest manifestation of that lack of understanding in which all sin takes its rise.

While a man is involved in sin he will condemn others who are likewise involved. And the deeper and greater his sin, the more severe will be his condemnation of others. It is only when a man begins to sorrow for his sin, and to rise above it into the clearer light of purity and understanding, that he ceases from condemning others and learns to sympathize with them.

But this ceaseless condemnation of each other by those who are involved in the fierce play of the passions is necessary, for it is one of the modes of operation of the Great Law which universally and eternally succeeds. Thus, the unrighteous one, who falls under the condemnation of others, will more rapidly reach a higher and nobler condition of heart and life if he humbly accepts the censure of others as the effect of his own sin. He then resolves henceforward to refrain from all condemnation of others.

The truly good and wise man, condemns none. Having put away all blind passion and selfishness he lives in the calm regions of love and peace. He understands all modes of sin, with their consequent sufferings and sorrows. Enlightened and awakened, freed from all selfish bias, he sees men as they are. His heart responds in holy sympathy with all. Should any condemn, abuse, or slander him, he surrounds them with the kindly protection of his sympathy. He sees the ignorance which prompts them to so act. He knows that they alone will suffer for their wrong acts.

Sympathy Evolves Through Suffering

Learn, by self-conquest and the acquisition of wisdom, to love him whom you now condemn, to Sympathize with those who condemn you. Turn your eyes away from condemnation and search your own heart, to find, perchance, some hard, unkind, or wrong thoughts which, when discovered and understood, you will condemn yourself.

Much that is commonly called sympathy is personal affection. To love them who love us is human bias and inclination; but to love them who do not love us is divine sympathy.

Compassion is needed because of the prevalence of suffering, for there is no being or creature who has not suffered. Through suffering sympathy is evolved. Not in a year or a life or an age is the human heart purified and softened by suffering. But after many lives of intermittent pain, after many ages of ever recurring sorrow, man reaps the golden harvest of his experiences, and garners in the rich, ripe fruits of love and wisdom. Then he understands, and by understanding, he sympathizes.

All suffering is the result of ignorantly violated

law, and after many repetitions of the same wrong act, and the same kind of suffering resulting from that act, knowledge of the law is acquired, and the higher state of obedience and wisdom is reached. Then there blossoms the pure and perfect flower of compassion.

The Desire to Alleviate Suffering

One aspect of sympathy is that of pity—pity for the distressed or pain-stricken, with a desire to alleviate or help them bear their sufferings. The world needs more of this divine quality.

> *"For pity makes the world*
> *Soft to the weak, and noble for the strong."*

But pity or compassion can only be developed by eradicating all hardness and unkindness, all accusation and resentment. He who sees another suffering for his sin, hardens his heart, and thinks or says: "It serves him right"—such a man cannot exercise pity nor apply the healing balm. Every time a man acts cruelly towards another (be it only a dumb creature), or refuses to bestow needed sympathy, he dwarfs himself, deprives himself of inexpressible blessedness, and prepares himself for suffering.

The Sympathy of Protecting Others

Another form of sympathy is that of rejoicing with those who are more successful than ourselves, as though their success were our own. Blessed indeed is he who is free from all envy and malice. He can rejoice and be glad when he hears of the good fortune of those who regard him as an enemy.

The protecting of creatures weaker and more indefensible than oneself is another form in which this divine sympathy is manifested. The helpless frailty of the dumb creation calls for the exercise of the deepest sympathy. The glory of superior strength resides in its power to shield, not to destroy. Not by the callous destruction of weaker things is life truly lived, but by their preservation:

*"All life
Is linked and kin."*

and the lowest creature is not separated from the highest but by greater weakness and by lesser intelligence.

When we pity and protect we reveal and enlarge the divine life and joy within ourselves. When we thoughtlessly or callously destroy, or inflict suffering, then our divine life becomes obscured, and its joy fades and dies. Bodies may feed bodies, and passions feed passions, but our divine nature is only nurtured, sustained, and developed by kindness, love, sympathy, and all pure and unselfish acts.

By bestowing sympathy on others we increase our own. Sympathy given can never be wasted. Even the meanest creature will respond to its heavenly touch, for it is the universal language which all creatures understand.

A Criminal Becomes Compassionate

I have recently heard a true story of a convict whose terms of incarceration in various prison terms extended to over forty years. As a criminal he was considered one of the most callous and hopelessly abandoned, and the wardens found him almost uncontrollable.

But one day he caught a mouse—a weak, terrified, hunted thing like himself. Its helpless frailty, and the similarity of its condition with his own, appealed to him, and ignited the divine spark of sympathy which smoldered in his crime-hardened heart, which no human touch had ever wakened into life.

He kept the mouse in an old boot in his cell, fed, tended, and loved it, and in his love for the weak and helpless he forgot and lost his hatred for the strong. His heart and his hand were no longer against his fellow inmates. He became docile and obedient to the utmost. The wardens could not understand his change. It seemed to them little short of miraculous that this most hardened of all criminals should suddenly be transformed into the likeness of a gentle, obedient child.

Even the expression of his features altered remarkably: a pleasing smile began to play around the mouth which had formerly been moved to nothing better than a cruel grin. And the implacable hardness of his eyes disappeared and gave place to a soft, deep, mellow light.

The criminal was a criminal no longer. He was saved, converted, clothed, and in his right mind. Restored to humaneness and to humanity, he set firmly on the pathway to divinity by pitying and caring for a defenseless creature. All this was made known to the prison officials shortly afterwards, when, on his discharge, he took the mouse away with him.

Compassion Is Blessedness Received

Thus compassion bestowed to others increases its store in our own hearts, and enriches and fructifies our

The Wisdom of James Allen III ~

own life. Sympathy given is blessedness received; sympathy withheld is blessedness forfeited. In the measure that a man increases and enlarges his compassion so much nearer does he approach the ideal life, the perfect blessedness. And when his heart has become so mellowed that no hard, bitter, or cruel thought can enter and detract from its permanent sweetness, then indeed is he richly and divinely blessed.

> *"When thy gaze*
> *Turns it on thine own soul, be most severe:*
> *But when it falls upon a fellow-man*
> *Let kindliness control it; and refrain*
> *From that belittling censure that springs forth*
> *From common lips like weeds from marshy soil."*
> —*Ella Wheeler Wilcox*

> *"I do not ask the wounded person how he feels,*
> *I myself become the wounded person."*
> —*Walt Whitman*

Forgiveness

THE REMEMBERING OF INJURIES is spiritual darkness; the fostering of resentment is spiritual suicide. To resort to the spirit and practice of forgiveness is the beginning of enlightenment. It is also the beginning of peace and happiness. There is no rest for him who broods over slights, injuries, and wrongs. Nor is there quiet repose of mind for him who feels that he has been unjustly treated, and who schemes how best to act to thwart the plans of his enemy.

How can happiness dwell in a heart that is so disturbed by ill-will? Do birds resort to a burning bush wherein to build and sing? Neither can happiness inhabit in that breast that is aflame with burning thoughts of resentment. Nor can wisdom come and dwell where such folly resides.

Revenge seems sweet only to the mind that is unacquainted with the spirit of forgiveness; but when the sweetness of forgiveness is tasted then the extreme bitterness of revenge is known. Revenge seems to lead to happiness to those who are involved in the darkness of passion. But when the violence of passion is abandoned, and the mildness of forgiveness is restored, then it is seen that revenge leads to suffering.

Revenge Is a Disease

Revenge is a virus which eats into the very vitals of the mind, and poisons the entire spiritual being. Resentment is a mental fever which burns up the wholesome energies of the mind, and "taking offense" is a form of moral sickness which saps the healthy flow of kindliness and good-will, and from which everyone should seek to be delivered.

The unforgiving and resentful spirit is a source of he who harbors and encourages it, who does not overcome and abandon it, forfeits much blessedness, and does not obtain any measure of true enlightenment. To be hard-hearted is to suffer and to be deprived of light and comfort. To be tender-hearted is to be serenely glad, to receive light and to be well comforted.

It will seem strange to many to be told that the

hard-hearted and unforgiving suffer most. Yet it is profoundly true, for not only do they, by the law of attraction, draw to themselves the revengeful passions in other people, but their hardness of heart itself is a continual source of suffering.

Hardness of Heart Brings Suffering

Every time a man hardens his heart against a fellow-being he inflicts upon himself five kinds of sufferings—namely, the suffering of lost communion and fellowship; the suffering of loss of love; the suffering of a troubled and confused mind; the suffering of wounded passion or pride; and the suffering of punishment inflicted by others.

Every act of unforgiveness entails upon the doer of that act these five sufferings; whereas every act of forgiveness brings to the doer five kinds of blessedness—namely, the blessedness of increased communion and fellowship; the blessedness of love; the blessedness of a calm and peaceful mind; the blessedness of passion stilled and pride overcome; and the blessedness, kindness, and good-will that is bestowed by others.

Numbers of people are today suffering the fiery torments of an unforgiving spirit, and only when they make an effort to overcome that spirit can they know what a cruel and exacting taskmaster they are serving. Only those who have abandoned the service of such a master for that of the nobler master of forgiveness can realize and know how grievous a service is the one, and how sweet the other.

Abandon Retaliation for Forgiveness

Let a man contemplate the strife of the world: how individuals and communities, neighbors and nations, live in continual retaliations towards each other. Let him realize the heartaches, the bitter tears, the grievous partings and misunderstandings—yea, even the blood-shed and woe which spring from that strife. And thus realizing, he will never again yield to ignoble thoughts or resentment, never again take offense at the actions of others, never again live in unforgiveness towards any being.

> *"Have good-will*
> *To all that lives, letting unkindness die,*
> *And greed and wrath; so that your lives be made*
> *Like soft airs passing by."*

When a man abandons retaliation for forgiveness he

passes from darkness to light. So dark and ignorant is unforgiveness that no being who is at all wise or enlightened could descend to it. But its darkness is not understood and known until it is left behind, and the better and nobler course of conduct is sought and practiced.

Man is blinded and deluded only by his own dark and sinful tendencies. The giving up of all unforgiveness means the giving up of pride and certain forms of passion, the abandonment of the deeply-rooted idea of the importance of oneself and of the necessity for protecting and defending that self. When that is done the higher life, greater wisdom, and pure enlightenment, which pride and passion completely obscured, are revealed in all their light and beauty.

Petty Resentments Fueled by Vanity

Then there are petty offenses, little spites and passing slights, which, while of a less serious nature than deep-seated hatreds and revenges, dwarf the character and cramp the soul. They are due to the sin of self and self-importance, and thrive on vanity. Whosoever is blinded and deluded by vanity will continually see something in the actions and the attitudes of others at which to take offense. And the more there is of vanity the more greatly will the imaginary slight or wrong be exaggerated. Moreover, to live in the frequent indulgence of petty resentments increases the spirit of hatred, and leads gradually downward to greater darkness, suffering, and self-delusion.

Don't take offense or allow your feelings to be hurt, which means—get rid of pride and vanity. Don't give occasion for offense or hurt the feelings of others, which means—be gently considerate, forgiving, and charitable towards all.

The giving up—the total uprooting—of vanity and pride is a great task; but it is a blessed task, and it can be accomplished by constant practice in non-resentment and by meditating upon one's thoughts and actions so as to understand and purify them. The spirit of forgiveness is perfected in one in the measure that pride and vanity are overcome and abandoned.

The not-taking-offense and the not-giving-offense go together. When a man ceases to resent the actions of others he is already acting kindly towards them, considering them before himself or his own defense. Such a man will be gentle in what he says and does. He will arouse love and kindness in others, and not stir them up to ill-will and strife. He will also be free from all fear concerning the actions of others towards him, for he who hurts none fears none.

But the unforgiving man, he who is eager to "pay back" some real or imaginary slight or injury, will not be considerate towards others, for he considers himself first, and is continually making enemies. He also lives in the fear of others, thinking that they are trying to do towards him as he is doing towards them. He who contrives the hurt of others fears others.

The Wisdom of Prince Dirghayu

There is a beautiful story of Prince Dirghayu which was told by an ancient Indian teacher to his disciples in order to impress them with the truth of the sublime precept that "hatred ceases not by hatred at any time; hatred ceases by non-hatred."

The story is as follows: Brahmadatta, a powerful king of Benares, made war upon Dirgheti, the king of Kosala, in order to annex his kingdom, which was much smaller than his own. Dirgheti, seeing that it was impossible for him to resist the greater power of Brahmadatta, fled, and left his kingdom in his enemy's hands. For some time he wandered from place to place in disguise, and at last settled down with his queen in an artisan's cottage. Eventually, the queen gave birth to a son, whom they called Dirghayu.

Now, King Brahmadatta was anxious to discover

the hiding-place of Dirgheti, in order to put to death the conquered king, for he thought, "Seeing that I have deprived him of his kingdom he may someday treacherously kill me if I do not kill him."

But many years passed away, and Dirgheti devoted himself to the education of his son, who by diligent application, became learned, skillful, and wise.

After a time Dirgheti's secret became known, and he, fearing that Brahmadatta would discover him and slay all three, and thinking more of the life of his son than his own, sent away the prince. Soon after the exiled king fell into the hands of Brahmadatta, and was, along with his queen, executed.

Now Brahmadatta thought: "I have got rid of Dirgheti and his queen, but their son, Prince Dirghayu, lives, and he will be sure to contrive some means of effecting my assassination. Yet he is unknown to any, and I have no means of discovering him." So the king lived in great fear and continual distress of mind.

Soon after the execution of his parents, Dirghayu, under an assumed name, sought employment in the king's stables, and was engaged by the master of elephants. Dirghayu quickly endeared himself to all, and his superior abilities came at last under the notice of the king, who had the young man brought before him. He was so charmed with him that he employed him in his own castle, and he proved to be so able and diligent that the king shortly placed him in a position of great trust under himself.

One day the king went on a long hunting expedition, and became separated from his attendants, Dirghayu alone remaining with him. And the king, being fatigued with his exertions, lay down, and slept with his head in Dirghayu's lap.

Then Dirghayu thought: "This king has greatly wronged me. He robbed my father of his kingdom, and slew my parents, and he is now entirely in my power." And he drew his sword, thinking to slay Brahmadatta. But, remembering how his father had taught him never to seek revenge but to forgive to the utmost, he sheathed his sword.

At last the king awoke out of a disturbed sleep, and the youth inquired of him why he looked so frightened. "My sleep," said the king, "is always restless, for I frequently dream that I am in the power of young Dirghayu and that he is about to slay me. While lying here I again dreamed that with greater vividness than ever before and it has filled me with dread and terror."

Then the youth, drawing his sword, said: "I am

Prince Dirghayu, and you are in my power: the time of vengeance has arrived."

Then the king fell upon his knees and begged Dirghayu to spare his life. And Dirghayu said: "It is you, O King! who must spare my life. For many years you have wished to find me in order that you might kill me; and, now that you have found me, let me beg of you to grant me my life."

And there and then did Brahmadatta and Dirghayu grant each other life, took hands, and solemnly vowed never to harm each other. And so overcome was the king by the noble and forgiving spirit of Dirghayu that he gave him his daughter in marriage, and restored to him his father's kingdom.

Forgiveness Is The Doorway to Love

Thus hatred ceases by non-hatred—by forgiveness, which is very beautiful, and is sweeter and more effective than revenge. It is the beginning of love, of that divine love that does not seek its own. And he who practices it, who perfects himself in it, comes at last to realize that blessed state wherein the torments of pride, vanity, hatred, and retaliation are forever dispelled. Then, good-will and peace become unchanging and unlimited.

In this state of calm, silent bliss, even forgiveness passes away, and is no longer needed. For he who reaches it sees no evil to resent but only ignorance and delusion on which to have compassion. Forgiveness is only needed so long as there is any tendency to resent, retaliate, and take offense. Equal love towards all is the perfect law, the perfect state in which all lesser states find their completion. Forgiveness is one of the doorways into the faultless temple of Divine Love.

> *"If men only understood*
> *All the emptiness and aching*
> *Of the sleeping and the waking*
> *Of the souls they judge so blindly,*
> *Of the hearts they pierce unkindly,*
> *They, with gentler words and feeling,*
> *Would apply the balm of healing—*
> *If they only understood."*

> *"Kindness, nobler ever than revenge."*
> —William Shakespeare

Seeing No Evil

AFTER MUCH PRACTICE in forgiveness and having cultivated the spirit of forgiveness up to a certain point, knowledge of the actual nature of good and evil dawns upon the mind. Then a man begins to understand how thoughts and motives are formed in the human heart, how they develop, and how take birth in the form of actions. This marks the opening of a new vision in the mind and the commencement of a nobler, higher, more divine life. For the man now begins to perceive that there is no necessity to resist or resent the actions of others towards him.

Whatever these actions may be, he will realize that all along his resentment has been caused by ignorance, and that his own bitterness of spirit is wrong. Having arrived thus far he will tax himself with such questions such as these: Why this continual retaliation and forgiveness? Why this tormenting anger against another and then this repentance and forgiveness? Is not forgiveness the taking back of one's anger, the giving up of one's resentment? And if anger and resentment are good and necessary why repent of them and give them up?

If it is so beautiful, so sweet, so peaceful to get rid of all feelings of bitterness and to utterly and wholly forgive, would it not be still more beautiful, sweet, and peaceful never to grow bitter at all, never to know anger, never to resent as evil the actions of another? Would it not be better to live in the experience of that pure, calm, blissful love which is known when an act of forgiveness is done, and all unruly passion towards another is put away?

If another has done me wrong is not my hatred towards him wrong, and can one wrong right another? Moreover, has he by his wrong really injured me, or has he injured himself? Am I not injured by my own wrong rather than by his? Why, then, do I grow angry? Why do I resent, retaliate, and engage in bitter thoughts? Is it not because my pride is offended or my vanity wounded or my selfishness thwarted? Is it not because my blind animal passions are aroused and allowed to subdue my better nature? Seeing that I am hurt by another person's attitude towards me because of my own pride, vanity, or ungoverned and unpurified passions, would it not be better to look to the wrong in myself rather than the wrong in another, to get rid of pride, vanity, and passion, and so avoid being hurt at all?

By such self-questionings and their elucidation in the light of serene thoughts and dispassionate conduct, a man, gradually overcoming passion and rising out of the ignorance which gives rise to passion, will at last reach that blessed state in which he will cease to see evil in others. He will dwell in universal goodwill, love, and peace.

Not that he will cease to see ignorance and folly; not that he will cease to see suffering, sorrow, and misery; not that he will cease to distinguish between acts that are pure and impure, right and wrong. For, having put away passion and prejudice, he will see these things in the full, clear light of knowledge, and exactly as they are. But he will cease to see anything—any evil power—in another which can do him injury, which he must violently oppose and strive to crush, and against which he must guard himself. Having arrived at a right understanding of evil by purging it away from his own heart, he sees that it is a thing that does not call for hatred, fear, and resentment but for consideration, compassion, and love.

Darkness Is The Absence of Light

Shakespeare through one of his characters says: "There is no darkness but ignorance."

All evil is ignorance, is dense darkness of mind, and the removal of sin from one's mind is a coming out of darkness into spiritual light.

Evil is the negation of good, just as darkness is the negation, or absence, of light, and what is there in a negation to arouse anger or resentment? When night settles down upon the world who is so foolish as to rail at the darkness? The enlightened man, likewise, does not accuse or condemn the spiritual darkness in men's hearts which is manifested in the form of sin, though by gentle reproof he may sometimes point out where the light lies.

Now the ignorance to which I refer as evil, or as the source of evil, is two-fold. There is wrong-doing which is committed without any knowledge of good and evil, and where there is no choice—this is unconscious wrong-doing. Then there is wrong-doing which is done in the knowledge that it ought not to be done—this is conscious wrong-doing. But both unconscious and conscious wrong-doing arise in ignorance—that is, ignorance of the real nature and painful consequences of the wrong-doing.

Pleasure and Pain Are One

Why does a man continue to do certain things which he feels he ought not to do? If he knows that what he is doing is wrong where lies the ignorance?

He continues to do those things because his knowledge of them is incomplete. He only knows he ought not to do them by certain precepts without and qualms of conscience within, but he does not fully and completely understand what he is doing. He knows that certain acts bring him immediate pleasure, and so, in spite of the troubled conscience which follows that pleasure, he continues to commit them. He is convinced that the pleasure is good and desirable, and therefore to be enjoyed. He does not know that pleasure and pain are one, but thinks he can have the one without the other.

This man has no knowledge of the law which governs human actions, and never thinks of associating his sufferings with his own wrong-doing. He believes that they are caused by the wrong-doing of others or are the mysterious dispensations of Providence, and therefore not to be inquired into or understood.

He is seeking happiness, and does those things which he believes will bring him most enjoyment, but he acts in entire ignorance of the hidden and inevitable consequences which attach to his actions.

Said a man to me once who was the victim of a bad habit: "I know the habit is a bad one, and that it does me more harm than good." I said: "If you know that what you are doing is bad and harmful why do you continue to do it?" And he replied: "Because it is pleasant, and I like it."

This man, of course, did not really know that his habit was bad. He had been told that it was, and he thought he knew or believed it was, but in reality he thought it was good, that it was conducive to his happiness and well-being. Therefore he continued to practice it.

When a man knows by experience that something is bad, and that every time he does it he injures body or mind, or both; when this knowledge is so complete that he is acquainted with its whole train of destructive effects, then he cannot do it any longer.

He cannot even desire to do it, and even the pleasure that was formerly in that thing becomes painful. No man would put a venomous snake in his pocket because it is prettily colored. One knows that a deadly sting lurks in those beautiful markings.

Likewise, when a man knows the unavoidable pain and hurt which lie hidden in wrong thoughts and actions, he does not continue to think and commit them. Even the immediate pleasure which he formerly sought with greed is gone from them. Their surface attractiveness has vanished. He is no longer ignorant concerning their true nature. He sees them as they are.

The Dishonest Businessman

I knew a young man who was in business, and although a member of a church, and occupying the position of a voluntary religious instructor, he told me that it was absolutely necessary to practice lying and deception in business, otherwise sure and certain ruin would follow. He said he knew lying was wrong, but while he remained in business he must continue to do it.

Upon questioning him I found, of course, that he had never tried truth and honesty in his business. He had not even thought of trying the better way, so firmly convinced was he that it was not a "better way," that it was not possible for him to know whether or not it would produce ruin.

Now, did this young man know that lying was wrong? There was a authoritative sense only in which he knew, but there was a deeper and more real sense in which he did not know. He had been taught to regard lying as wrong, and his conscience bore out that teaching, but he believed that it brought to him profit, prosperity, and happiness, and that honesty would bring him loss, poverty, and misery. In a word, he regarded lying, deep in his heart, as the right thing to do, and honesty as the wrong practice.

He had no knowledge whatever of the real nature of the act of lying: how it *is*, on the instant of its committal, loss of character, loss of self-respect, loss of power, usefulness, and influence, and loss of blessedness; and how it unerringly leads to loss of reputation and loss of material profit and prosperity.

Only when such a man begins to consider happiness of others, and prefers to embrace the loss which he fears rather than clutch at the gain which he desires, will he obtain that real knowledge which lofty moral conduct alone can reveal. And then, experiencing the greater blessedness, he will see how, all along, he has been deceiving and defrauding himself rather than others. He has been living in darkest ignorance and self-delusion.

Sin Is a Condition of Ignorance

These two common instances of wrong-doing will serve to illustrate and make plainer, to those of my readers who, while searching for Truth, are as yet doubtful, uncertain, and confused. The deep Truth is that all sin, or evil, is a condition of ignorance and therefore to be dealt with in a loving and not a hateful spirit.

And as with bad habits and lying, so with all sin—with lust, hatred, malice, envy, pride, vanity, self-indulgence and selfishness in all its forms; it is a state of spiritual darkness, the absence of the Light of Truth in the heart, the negation of knowledge.

Thus when, by overcoming the wrong condition in one's own heart, the nature of evil is fully realized, and mere belief gives place to living knowledge, evil can no longer be hatefully condemned and violently resisted, and the wrong-doer is thought of with tender compassion.

The Desire to Convert Others

This brings us to another aspect of evil—namely, that of individual freedom; the right of every person to choose his own actions. Along with the seeing of evil in

The Wisdom of James Allen III ~

A Measure of Light and Darkness

The truly wise and good man sees good in all, evil in none. He has abandoned the folly of wanting others to think and act as he thinks and acts, for he sees that men are variously constituted. He understands that they are at different points in their spiritual evolution, and must, of necessity, think and act differently. Having put away hatred, condemnation, egotism, and prejudice he has become enlightened, and sees that purity, love, compassion, gentleness, patience, humility, and unselfishness are manifestations of light and knowledge; while impurity, hatred, cruelty, passion, anger, pride, and selfishness are manifestations of darkness and ignorance.

He sees that whether men are living in light or darkness, they are one and all doing that which they think is necessary. Everyone is acting in accordance with their own measure of light or darkness. The wise understands, and, with this understanding, ceases from all bitterness and accusation.

Every man acts in accordance with his nature, with his own sense of right and wrong, and is surely gathering in the results of his own experience. There is one supreme right which every being possesses— the right to think and act as he chooses.

others is the desire to convert or coerce others into one's own ways of thinking and acting. Probably the commonest delusion in which men are involved is that of thinking that what they themselves believe, think, and do is good, and all that is otherwise is evil, and therefore to be powerfully condemned and resisted. It is out of this delusion that all persecutions spring.

There are Christians who regard all atheists as wholly evil, as given up to the service of an evil power. And there are atheists who firmly believe that all Christians are doing the greatest harm to the whole human race by their "superstitious and false doctrines." The truth is that neither the Christian nor the atheist is evil, nor in the service of evil, but each is choosing his own way, and is pursuing that course which he is convinced is right.

Let a man quietly contemplate the fact that numbers of followers of various religions the world over are, as they ever were, engaged in condemning each other as evil and wrong, while regarding themselves as good and right. This will help him to realize how all evil is merely ignorance and spiritual darkness. Earnest meditation on that fact will be found to be one of the greatest aids in developing greater kindness, charity, insight and breadth of mind.

If he chooses to think and act selfishly, thinking of his own immediate happiness only and not of that of others, then he will rapidly bring upon himself, by the action of the moral law of cause and effect, such afflictions as will cause him to pause and consider, and so find a better way.

Eliminating Judgement by Love

There is no teacher to compare with experience, no chastisement so corrective and purifying as that which men ignorantly inflict upon themselves. The selfish man is the ignorant man. He chooses his own way, but it is a way which leads to suffering, and through suffering to knowledge and bliss. The good man is the wise man; he likewise chooses his own way. But he chooses it in the full light of knowledge. Having passed through the stages of ignorance and suffering, he has arrived at wisdom and bliss.

A man begins to understand what "seeing no evil" is when, putting away all personal desires in his judgement of others, he considers them from their own standpoint. He judges their actions not from his own standard but from theirs.

It is because men set up arbitrary standards of right and wrong, and are anxious that all should conform to their particular standard, that they see evil in each other.

A man is only rightly judged when he is judged not from my standard or yours but from his own, and to deal with him thus is not a judgement—it is Love. It is only when we look through the eyes of Impersonal Love that we become enlightened, and see others as they really are.

A man is approaching that Love when he can say in his heart: "Who am I that I should judge another? Am I so pure and sinless that I arraign men and pass the judgement of evil upon them? Rather let me humble myself, and correct my own errors, before assuming the position of supreme judge of those of other men."

Casting The First Stone

It was said by one of old to those who were about to stone, as evil, a woman taken in the act of committing a dark sin: "He that is without sin let him cast the first stone." And though he who said it was without sin yet he took up no stone, nor passed any bitter judgement, but said, with infinite gentleness and compassion: "Neither do I condemn thee. Go, and sin no more."

In the pure heart there is no room left where personal judgements and hatreds can find lodging, for it is filled to overflowing with tenderness and love. The pure heart sees no evil. And only as men succeed in seeing no evil in others will they become free from sin, sorrow, and suffering.

No man sees evil in himself or his own acts except the man who is becoming enlightened, and then he abandons those acts which he has come to see are wrong. Every man justifies himself in what he does, and, however evil others may regard his conduct, he himself thinks it to be good and necessary. If he did not he would not, could not, do it.

The Base Conduct of The Ignorant

The angry man always justifies his anger; the covetous man his greed; the impure man his unchastity. The liar considers that his lying is altogether necessary. The slanderer believes that, in defaming the characters of those whom he dislikes, and warning other people against their "evil" natures, he is doing well. The thief is convinced that stealing is the shortest and best way to plenty, prosperity, and happiness. And even the murderer thinks that there is a ground of justification for his deed.

Every man's deeds are in accordance with the measure of his own light or darkness, and no man can live higher than he is or act beyond the limits of his knowledge. Nevertheless, he can improve himself, and thereby gradually increase his light and extend the range of his knowledge.

The angry man indulges in ridicule and abuse because his knowledge does not extend to forbearance and patience. Not having practiced gentleness, he does not understand it, and cannot choose it. Nor can he know, by its comparison with the light of gentleness, the darkness of anger. It is the same with the liar, the slanderer, and the thief. They live in this dark condition of mind and action because they are limited to it by their immature knowledge and experience. Never having lived in the higher conditions, they have no knowledge of them, and it is, to them, as if they were non-existent.

"The light shineth in the darkness and the darkness comprehendeth it not." Nor can they understand even the conditions in which they are living, because, being dark, they are necessarily devoid of all knowledge.

Reflecting Upon Your Conduct

When a man is driven by repeated sufferings to at last reflect upon his conduct, he comes to see that his anger or lying, or whatever ignorant condition he may have been living in, is productive only of trouble and sorrow. Then he abandons it, and begins to search for, and practice, the opposite and enlightened condition. When he is firmly established in the better way, so that his knowledge of both conditions is complete, then he realizes in what great darkness he had formerly lived. This knowledge of good and evil by experience constitutes enlightenment.

When a man begins to look, as it were, through the eyes of others, and to measure them by their own standard and not by his, then he ceases from seeing the evil in others, for he knows that every man's perception and standard of good and evil is different. He knows that there is no vice so low but some men regard it as good; no virtue so high but some men regard it as evil. What a man regards as good that to him is good; what he regards as evil that to him is evil.

Nor will the purified man, who has ceased to see evil in others, have any desire to win others to his own ways or opinions. Rather, he will help them in their own particular groove, knowing that an enlarged experience only, and not merely change of opinion can lead to higher knowledge and greater blessedness.

It will be found that men see evil in those who differ from them and good in those who agree with them. The man who greatly loves himself and is enamored of his opinions will love all those who agree with him and will dislike all those who disagree with him. "If ye love them that love ye, what reward have ye?... Love your enemies, do good to them that hate you."

Inflicting Cruelty on Others

Egotism and vanity make men blind. Men of opposing religious views hate and persecute each other. Men of opposing political views fight and condemn each other. The partisan measures all men by his own standard, and sets up his judgements accordingly. So convinced is he that he is right and others wrong that he at last persuades himself that to inflict cruelty on others is both good and necessary in order to coerce them into his way of thinking and acting, and so bring them to the right—his right—against their own reason and will.

Men hate, condemn, resist, and inflict suffering upon each other, not because they are intrinsically evil, and not because they are deliberately "wicked." They are doing, in the full light of truth, what they know to be wrong, yet they regard such conduct as necessary and right. All men are intrinsically good, but some are wiser than others and are older in experience than others.

~ Byways of Blessedness

A Dialogue Between Two Men

I recently heard, in substance, the following conversation between two men whom I will call D and E. The third person referred to as X is a prominent politician:

E: Every man reaps the result of his own thoughts and deeds, and suffers for his own wrong.

D: If that is so, and if no man can escape from the penalty of his evil deeds, what an inferno some of our men in power must be preparing for themselves.

E: Whether a man is in power or not, so long as he lives in ignorance and sin, he will reap sorrow and suffering.

D: Look, for instance, at X, a man totally evil, given up entirely to selfishness and ambition. Surely great torments are reserved for so unprincipled a man.

E: But how do you know he is so evil?

D: By his works, his fruits. When I see a man doing evil, I know that he is evil; and I cannot even think of X but I burn with righteous indignation. I am sometimes inclined to doubt that there is an overruling power for good when I see such a man in a position where he can do so much harm to others.

E: What evil is he committing?

D: His whole policy is evil. He will ruin the country if he remains in power.

E: But while there are large numbers of people who think of X as you do, there are also large numbers, equally intelligent, who look upon him as good and able, who admire him for his excellent qualities, and regard his policy as beneficent and making for national progress. He owes his position to these people. Are they also evil?

D: They are deceived and misled. And this only makes X's evil all the greater, in that he can so successfully employ his talents in deceiving others in order to gain his own selfish ends. I hate the man.

E: May it not be possible that you are deceived?

D: In what way?

E: Hatred is self-deception; love is self-enlightenment. No man can see either himself or others clearly until he ceases from hatred and practices love.

D: That sounds very beautiful, but it is impracticable. When I see a man doing evil to others, and deceiving and misleading them, I must hate him. It is right that I should do so. X is without a spark of conscience.

E: X may or may not be all you believe him to be, but, even if he is, according to your own words, he should be pitied and not condemned.

D: How so?

E: You say he is without a conscience.

D: Entirely so.

E: Then he is a mental cripple. Do you hate the blind because they cannot see, the dumb because they cannot speak, or the deaf because they cannot hear? When a captain has lost his rudder or broken his compass do you condemn him because he did not keep his ship off the rocks? Do you hold him responsible for the loss of life?

If a man is totally devoid of conscience he is without the means of moral guidance, and all his selfishness must, by necessity, appear to him good, right, and proper. X may appear evil to you, but is he evil to himself? Does he regard his own conduct as evil?

D: Whether he regards himself as evil or not he is evil.

E: If I were to regard you as evil because of your hatred for X should I be right?

D: No.

E: Why not?

D: Because in such a case hatred is necessary, justifiable, and righteous. There is such a thing as righteous anger, righteous hatred.

E: Is there such a thing as righteous selfishness, righteous ambition, righteous evil? I should be quite wrong in regarding you as evil, because you are doing what you are convinced is right, because you regard your hatred for X as part of your duty as a man and a citizen. Nevertheless, there is a better way than that of hatred, and it is the knowledge of this better way that prevents me from hating X as you do, because however wrong his conduct might appear to me, it is not wrong to him, nor to his supporters. Moreover, all men reap as they sow.

D: What, then, is that better way?

E: It is the way of Love; the ceasing to regard others as evil. It is a blessed and peaceful state of heart.

D: Do you mean that there is a state which a man can reach wherein he will not grow angry when he sees people doing evil?

E: No, I do not mean that, for while a man regards others as evil he will continue to grow angry with them; but I mean that a man can reach a state of calm insight and spotless love wherein he sees no evil to grow angry with, wherein he understands the various natures of men—how they are prompted to act, and how they reap, as the harvest of their own thoughts and deeds, the weeds of suffering and the fruit of bliss. To reach that state is to regard all men and women with compassion and love.

D: The state that you picture is a very high one—it is, no doubt, a very holy and beautiful one—but it is a state that I should be sorry to reach; and I should pray to be preserved from a state of mind wherein I could not hate a man like X with an intense hatred.

Thus by this conversation it will be seen that D regarded his hatred as good. Even so all men regard that which they do as necessary to be done. The things which men habitually practice, those things they believe in. When faith in a thing wholly ceases it ceases to be practiced. D's individual liberty is equal to that of other men, and he has a right to hate another if he so wishes. Nor will he abandon his hatred until he discovers, by the sorrow and unrest which it entails, how wrong, foolish, and blind it is, and how, by its practice, he is injuring himself.

Evil Is Wrongly Directed Energy

A great Teacher was once asked by one of His disciples to explain the distinction between good and evil, and, holding His hand with the fingers pointing downward, He said: "Where is my hand pointing?"

The disciple replied: "It is pointing downward."

Then, turning His hand upward, the Teacher

asked: "Where now is my hand pointing?"

And the disciple answered: "It is pointing upward."

"That," said the Teacher, "is the distinction between evil and good."

By this simple illustration He indicated that evil is merely wrongly-directed energy, and good rightly-directed energy, and that the so-called evil man becomes good by reversing his conduct.

To understand the true nature of evil by living in the good is to cease to see other men as evil. Blessed is he who, turning from the evil in others exerts himself in the purification of his own heart. He shall one day become of "too pure eyes to behold evil."

The Brotherhood of Humanity

Knowing the nature of evil, what is appropriate for a man to do? It is necessary to live only in that which is good. Therefore, if a man condemns me, I will not condemn him in return. If he reviles me, I will give him kindness. If he slanders me, I will speak of his good qualities. If he hates me then he greatly needs, and shall receive, my love. With the impatient I will be patient. With the greedy I will be generous. And with the violent and quarrelsome I will be mild and peaceable. Seeing no evil, whom should I hate or who regard as mine enemy?

> "Were mankind murderous or jealous upon you,
>   my brother, my sister?
> I'm so sorry for you. They are not murderous
>   or jealous upon me;
> All has been gentle with me, I keep no account
>   with lamentation;
> What have I to do with lamentation?"

He who sees men as evil imagines that behind those acts which are called "wicked" there is a corporate and substantial evil prompting those particular sins. But he of stainless vision sees the deeds themselves as the evil, and knows that there is no evil power, no evil soul or man behind those deeds. The substance of the universe is good; there is no substance of evil. Good alone is permanent; there is no fixed or permanent evil.

Brothers and sisters, born of the same parents and being of one household, love each other through all adversity. They see no evil in each other, but overlook all errors, and cling together in the strong bonds of affection. Even so the good man sees humanity as one spiritual family, born of the same Father-Mother, being of the same essence and making for the same goal. He regards all men and women as brothers and sisters and makes no divisions and distinctions. He sees none as evil, but is at peace with all. Happy is he who attains this blessed state.

> *"The solid, solid universe*
> *Is pervious to Love;*
> *With bandaged eyes he never errs,*
> *Around below, above.*
> *His blinding light*
> *He flingeth white*
> *On God's and Satan's brood,*
> *And reconciles*
> *By mystic wiles*
> *The evil and the good."*
> —*Emerson*

> *"If thou thinketh evil, be thou sure*
> *Thine acts will bear the shadow of the stain;*
> *And if thy thought be perfect, then thy deed*
> *Will be as perfect, true and pure."*
> —*After Confucius*

Abiding Joy

ABIDING JOY! Is there such a thing? Where is it? Who possesses it? Yea; there is such a thing. It is where there is no sin and error. It is possessed by the pure hearted.

As darkness is a passing shadow, and light is substance that remains, so sorrow is fleeting, but joy abides forever. No true thing can pass away and become lost; no false thing can remain and be preserved. Sorrow is false, and it cannot live; joy is true, and it cannot die. Joy may become hidden for a time, but it can always be recovered; sorrow may remain for a period, but it can be transcended and dispersed.

Do not think your sorrow will remain; it will pass away like a cloud. Do not believe that the torments of sin are ever your portion; they will vanish like a hideous nightmare. Awake! Arise! Be holy and joyful!

You are the creator of your own shadows; you desire and then you grieve; renounce and then you shall rejoice. You are not the impotent slave of sorrow. The never-ending Happiness awaits your Homecoming. You are not the helpless prisoner of the darkness who dreams of sin. Even now the beautiful light of holiness shines upon your sleeping lids, ready to greet your awakening vision.

When Sin Is Abandoned, Joy Is Found

In the heavy, troubled sleep of sin and self the abiding joy is lost and forgotten. Its undying music is no more heard, and the fragrance of its fadeless flowers no longer cheers the heart of the wayfarer.

But when sin and self are abandoned, when the clinging to things for personal pleasure is put away, then the shadows of grief disappear, and the heart is restored to its Imperishable Joy.

Joy comes and fills the self-emptied heart. It abides with the peaceful; its reign is with the pure.

Joy flees from the selfish. It deserts the quarrelsome; it is hidden from the impure.

Joy is as an angel so beautiful, delicate, and chaste

that she can only dwell with holiness. She cannot remain with selfishness; she is wedded to Love.

Joy is revealed just in the measure that selfish desire is put away. And although the full, living consciousness of its abidingness, the unbroken continuance of its presence from moment to moment, is reserved only for the altogether pure, its sweetness is tasted by all in their moments and hours of exaltation. In every truly unselfish thought and act, the joy which is not excitement, not that feverish thing called pleasure, and which is followed by no tearful reaction, is revealed.

Every man is truly happy in so far as he is unselfish. He is miserable in so far as he is selfish. All truly good men, and by good men I mean all those who have fought victoriously the battle against self, are blessed of joy. How great is the jubilation of the saint!

All Becoming Is Painful

No true teacher promises sorrow as the ultimate of life; he promises joy. He points to sorrow, but only as a process which sin has rendered necessary. Where the ego-self ends—grief passes away. Joy is the companion of righteousness. In the divine life tender compassion fills the place where weeping sorrow sat.

During the process of becoming unselfish there are periods of deep sorrow. Purification is necessarily severe. All becoming is painful. Abiding joy in its completion is realized only in the perfection of being, and this is:

> *"A state*
> *Where all is loveliness, and power and love,*
> *With all sublimest qualities of mind,*
> *Where all*
> *Enjoy entire dominion o'er themselves.*
> *Acts, feelings, thoughts, conditions qualities."*

Life Is Similar to a Flower Growing

Consider how a flower evolves and becomes. At first there is a little germ groping its way in the dark soil towards the upper light; then the plant appears, and leaf is added unto leaf. Finally the perfected flower appears, in the sweet perfume and virgin beauty of which all effort ceases.

So, with human life. At first there is a blind groping for the light in the dark soil of selfishness and ignorance. Then there is the coming into the light, and the gradual overcoming of selfishness with its accompanying pain and sorrow. Finally blooms the perfect flower of a pure, unselfish life, giving forth, without effort, the perfume of holiness and the beauty of joy.

The good, the pure, are the superlatively happy. However others may argumentatively deny or qualify this, humanity instinctively knows it to be true. Do not men everywhere picture their angels as the most joyful of beings? There are joyful angels in bodies of flesh; we meet them and pass on. And how many of those who come in contact with them are sufficiently pure to see vision within the form—to see the incorruptible angel in its common instrument of clay?

> *"They needs must grope who cannot see,*
> *The blade before the ear must be;*
> *The outward symbols disappear*
> *From him whose inward sight is clear."*

Yes; the pure are the joyful. We look almost in vain for any expressions of sorrow in the words of Jesus. The "Man of Sorrows" is only completed in the Man of Joy:

> *"I, Buddha, who wept with all my brother's tears,*
> *Whose heart was broken by a whole world's woe,*
> *Laugh and am glad, for there is Liberty!"*

In sin, and in the struggle against sin, there is unrest and affliction, but in the perfection of Truth, in the path of Righteousness, there is abiding joy.

> *"Enter the Path! There spring the healing streams*
> *Quenching all thirst! There bloom immortal flowers*
> *Carpeting all the way with joy! There throng*
> *Swiftest and sweetest hours!"*

What Is The "Good News"?

Tribulation lasts only so long as there remains some chaff of self which needs to be removed. The threshing-machine ceases to work when all the grain is separated from chaff; and when the last impurities are blown away from the soul, suffering has completed its work, and there is no more need for it. Then abiding joy is realized.

All the saints, prophets, and saviors of the race have proclaimed with rejoicing the "Gospel," or the "Good News." All men know what Good News is—an impending calamity avoided, a disease cured, friends arrived or returned in safety, difficulties overcome, success in some enterprise assured—but what is the "Good News" of the saintly ones?

This: that there is peace for the troubled, healing

for the afflicted, gladness for the grief-stricken, victory for the sinful, a homecoming for the wanderer, and joy for the sorrowing and broken-hearted. Not that these beautiful realities shall be in some future world, but that they are here and now, that they are known, realized, and enjoyed. They are, therefore, proclaimed so that all may accept them who will break the galling bonds of self and rise into the glorious liberty of unselfish love.

The Sanctuary of Joy Is Within

Seek the highest Good, and as you find it, as you practice it and realize it, you will taste the deepest, sweetest joy. As you succeed in forgetting your own selfish desires in your thoughtfulness for others, in your care for others, in your service for others, just so far and no further, will you find and realize the abiding joy in life.

Inside the gateway of unselfishness lies the sanctuary of Abiding Joy, and whosoever will may enter in, whosoever doubts let him come and see.

And knowing this—that selfishness leads to misery, and unselfishness to joy, not merely for one's self alone—for if this were all, how unworthy would be our endeavors!—but for the whole world, and because all with whom we live and come in contact will be the happier and truer for our unselfishness.

Humanity is one, and the joy of one is the joy of all. Knowing this let us scatter flowers and not thorns in the common ways of life. Yea, even in the highway of our enemies let us scatter the blossoms of unselfish love—so shall the pressure in their footprints fill the air with the perfume of holiness and gladden the world with the aroma of joy.

> *"Who will carry music in their heart*
> *Through dusky lane and wrangling mart,*
> *Plying their daily toil with busier feet,*
> *Because their secret souls a holier strain repeat."*
> —Keble

> *"Serene will be our days and bright,*
> *And happy will our nature be,*
> *When love is an unerring light,*
> *And joy its own security."*
> —Wordsworth

Silentness

IN THE WORDS OF A WISE MAN there is great power, but his silence is more powerful still. The greatest teachers teach us most effectively when they are purposely silent. The silent attitude of the great man, noted, perhaps, by one or two of his disciples only, is recorded and preserved through the ages. Whereas, the obtrusive words of the merely clever talker, heard, perhaps, by thousands, and at once popularized, are neglected and forgotten in, at most, a few generations.

The silence of Jesus, when asked by Pilate "What is Truth?" is the impressive, the awful silence of profound wisdom. It is pregnant with humility and reproof. It perpetually rebukes that shallowness which, illustrating the truth that "fools step in where angels fear to tread," would parcel out the universe in terms of triteness, or think to utter the be-all and end-all of the mystery of things in some textual formula or theological platitude.

When, plied with questions about Brahma (God) by the argumentative Brahmans, Buddha remained silent, he taught them better than they knew, and if by his silence he failed to satisfy the foolish he thereby profoundly instructed the wise.

Why all this ceaseless talk about God, with its accompaniment of intolerance? Let men practice some measure of kindliness and good-will, and thereby acquaint themselves with the simple rudiments of wisdom. Why all these speculative arguments about the nature of God? Let us first understand somewhat of ourselves. There are no greater marks of folly and moral immaturity than irreverence and presumption; no greater manifestations of wisdom and moral maturity than reverence and humility.

Lao-Tze, in his own life, exemplified his teaching that the wise man "teaches without words." Disciples were attracted to him by the power which ever accompanies a wise reserve. Living in comparative obscurity and silence, not courting the ear of men, and never going out to teach, men sought him out and learned of him wisdom.

The Masters of Silence

The silent acts of the Great Ones are beacons to

the wise, illuminating their pathway with no uncertain radiance, for he who would attain to virtue and wisdom must learn, not only when to speak and what to say, but also when to remain silent and what not to say. The right control of the tongue is the beginning of wisdom; the right control of the mind is the consummation of wisdom. By curbing his tongue a man gains possession of his mind, and to have complete possession of one's mind is to be a Master of Silence.

The fool babbles, gossips, argues, and bandies words. He glories in the fact that he has had the last word and has silenced his opponent. He exults in his own folly, is ever on the defensive, and wastes his energies in unprofitable channels. He is like a gardener who continues to dig and plant in unproductive soil.

The wise man avoids idle words, gossip, vain argument, and self-defense. He is content to appear defeated. He rejoices when he is defeated, knowing that, having found and removed another error in himself, he has thereby become wiser. Blessed is he who does not strive for the last word!

*"Backward I see in my own days where I sweated
through fog with linguists and contenders;
I have no mockings or arguments, I witness and wait."*

Silence under provocation is the mark of a cultured and sympathetic soul. The thoughtless and unkind are stirred by every slight provocation, and will lose their mental balance by even the appearance of a personal encroachment.

The self-possession of Jesus is not a miracle; it is the flower of culture, the crown of wisdom. When we read of Jesus that "He answered never a word" and of Buddha that "He remained silent," we get a glimpse of the vast power of silence, of the silent majesty of true greatness.

Strength in Silence

The silent man is the powerful man. The victim of annoying talkativeness is devoid of influence; his spiritual energies are dissipated. Every mechanic knows that before a force can be utilized and definitely directed it must be conserved and stored. The wise man is a spiritual mechanic who conserves the energies of his mind, holds them in masterful suspension, ready at any moment to direct them, with effective purpose, to the accomplishment of some necessary work.

The true strength is in silentness. It is well said that "The dog that barks does not bite." The grim and rarely broken silence of the bull-dog is the necessary adjunct to that powerfully concentrated and effectual action for which the animal is known and feared. This, of course, is a lower form of silentness, but the principle is the same.

The braggart fails. His mind is diverted from the main purpose; and his energies are frittered away upon self-glorification. His forces are divided between his task and the reward to himself, the greater portion going to feed the lust of reward. He is like an unskillful general who loses the battle through dividing his forces instead of concentrating them upon a point. Or he is like a careless engineer who leaves open the waste-valve of his engine and allows the steam to run down.

The modest, silent, earnest man succeeds. Freed from vanity, and avoiding the dissipation of self-glorification, all his powers are concentrated upon the successful performance of his task. Even while the other man is talking about his powers he is already about his work, and is so much nearer than the other to its completion. It is a law everywhere and always that energy distributed is subject unto energy conserved. The noisy and boastful will ever be overthrown by the quiet and modest. It is a law universally applicable that quietness is strength.

Silence Is a Corollary to Success

The business man who succeeds never talks

about his plans, methods, and affairs, and should he, turned giddy by success, begin to do this he will then commence to fail.

The man of great moral influence never talks about himself and his spiritual victories, for, should he do so, in that moment his moral power and influence would be gone, and, like Samson, he would be shorn of strength. Success, worldly or spiritual, is the willing servant of strong, steady, silent, unflinching purpose. The most powerful disintegrating forces make no noise. The greatly-overcoming mind works silently.

If you would be strong, useful, and self-reliant learn the value and power of silentness. Do not talk about yourself. The world instinctively knows that the vain talker is weak and empty, and so it leaves him to his own vanity. Do not talk about what you are going to do but do it! Let your finished work speak for itself.

Do not waste your forces in criticizing and disparaging the work of others but set about to do your own work thoroughly and well. The worst work with earnestness and sweetness behind it is altogether better than barking at others. While you are disparaging the work of others you are neglecting your own. If others are doing badly help and instruct them by doing better yourself. Neither abuse others nor place any value on their abusive ways. When attacked remain silent. In this way you will conquer yourself, and will, without the use of words, teach others.

The Silent Mind

But the true silence is not merely a silent tongue; it is a silent mind. To merely hold one's tongue, and yet to carry about a disturbed and rankling mind, is no remedy for weakness and no source of power. Silentness, to be powerful, must envelop the whole mind, must permeate every chamber of the heart. It must be the silence of peace.

In the measure that a man conquers himself is this broad, deep, abiding silentness attained. While passions, temptations, and sorrows disturb, the holier, profounder depths of silence are yet to be sounded. To smart or feel stinging distress under the words and actions of others means that you are still weak, uncontrolled, and unpurified. Rid your heart of the disturbing influences of vanity, pride, and selfishness so that no petty spite can reach you, so no slander or abuse can disturb your serene repose.

As the storm rages ineffectually against a well-built house, while its occupant sits composed and happy by his fireplace within, so no evil without can disturb or harm him who is well fortified with wisdom; self-governed and silent. He remains at peace within. To this great silence the self-conquered person attains.

> *"Envy and calumny, and hate and pain,*
> *And that unrest which men miscall delight,*
> *Can touch him not, nor torture him again."*

Talking Dissipates Strength

There is no commoner error amongst men than that of supposing that nothing can be accomplished without much talking and much noise. The busy, shallow talker regards the quiet thinker or silent doer as a man wasted. He thinks silentness means "doing nothing," and that hurrying, bustling, and ceaseless talking means "doing much." He also confounds popularity with power.

The thinker and doer is the real and effectual worker. His work is at the root, core, and substance of things. And as Nature silently, yet with hidden and wondrous alchemy, transmutes the rude elements of earth and air into tender leaves, beautiful flowers, delectable fruits,—yea, into abundant forms of beauty—even so does the silent purposeful worker transform the ways of men and the face of the world by the might and magic of his silently directed energy.

He wastes no time and force in tinkering with the ever-changing and artificial surface of things, but goes to the living vital center. He works therefrom and thereon. In due season, perhaps when his perishable form is withdrawn from the world, the fruits of his obscure but imperishable labors come forth to gladden the world. But the words of the talker perish. The world reaps no harvest from the sowing of sound.

The Silence of The Quakers

He who conserves his mental forces also conserves his physical forces. The strongly quiet, calm man lives to a greater age, and in the possession of better health than the hurrying, noisy man. Quiet, subdued mental harmony is conducive to physical harmony—health.

The Quakers are today the healthiest, longest-lived and most successful portion of the British community, and they live quiet, simple, and purposeful lives, avoiding all worldly excitements and unnecessary words. They are a silent people. All their meetings are conducted on the principle that "Silence is Power."

Silentness is powerful because it is the outcome of self-conquest, and the more successfully a man governs himself the more silent he becomes. As he succeeds in living for a purpose, and not for the pleasures of self, he withdraws himself from the outer discord of the world and reaches to the inward music of peace. Then when he speaks there is purpose and power behind his words. And when he maintains silence there is equal or even greater power therein.

He does not utter that which is followed by pain and tears. He does not do that which is productive of sorrow and remorse. But, saying and doing those things only which are ripe with thoughtfulness, his conscience is quiet, and all his days are blessed.

> *"Why idly seek from outward things*
> *The answer inward silence brings?*
> *Why climb the far-off hills with pain,*
> *A nearer view of heaven to gain?*
> *In the lowliest depths of bosky dells*
> *The hermit contemplation dwells,*
> *Whence, piercing heaven, with screened sight,*
> *He sees at noon the stars, whose light*
> *Shall glorify the coming night."*
> — Whittier

*"In the still hour when passion is at rest,
Gather up stores of wisdom in thy breast."*
— Wordsworth

*"Be still! The crown of life is silentness.
Give thou a quiet hour to each long day,
Too much of time we spend in profitless
And foolish talk. Too little do we say.*

*If thou wouldst gather words that shall avail,
Learning a wisdom worthy to express,
Leave for a while thy chat and empty tale—
Study the golden speech of silentness."*
— A. L. Salmon

*"Be still, my soul.
Rest awhile from the feverish activities
   in which you lose yourself.
Be not afraid to be left alone with yourself
   for one short hour."*
— Ernest Crosby

Solitude

MAN'S ESSENTIAL BEING is inward, invisible, spiritual, and as such it derives its life and strength, from within, not from without. Outward things are channels through which its energies are expended, but for renewal it must fall back on the inward silence.

In so far as man strives to drown this silence in the noisy pleasures of the senses, and endeavors to live in the conflicts of outward things, just so much does he reap the experiences of pain and sorrow. But when these become at last intolerable, they drive him back to the feet of the inward Comforter, to the shrine of the peaceful solitude within.

As the body cannot thrive on empty husks, neither can the spirit be sustained on empty pleasures. If not regularly fed the body loses its vitality, and, pained with hunger and thirst, cries out for food and drink. It is the same with the spirit. It must be regularly nourished in solitude on pure and holy thoughts or it will lose its freshness and strength, and will at last cry out in its painful and utter starvation.

The yearning of an anguished-stricken soul for light and consolation is the cry of a spirit that is perishing of hunger and thirst. All pain and sorrow is spiritual starvation, and aspiration is the cry for spiritual food. It is the Prodigal Son who, perishing of hunger, turns his face longingly towards his Father's home.

Solitude Is Indispensable

The pure life of the spirit cannot be found, but is lost, in the life of the senses. The lower desires are ever clamorous for more, and they afford no rest. The outward world of pleasure, personal contact, and noisy activities is a sphere of wear and tear which necessitates the counterbalancing effect of solitude.

Just as the body requires rest for the recuperation of its forces, so the spirit requires solitude for the renewal of its energies. Solitude is as indispensable to spiritual welfare as sleep is to bodily well-being. And pure thought, or meditation, which is evoked in solitude, is to the spirit what activity is to the body.

As the body breaks down when deprived of the needful rest and sleep, so do the spirits of men break down, being deprived of the necessary silence and solitude. Man, as a spiritual being, cannot be maintained in strength, uprightness, and peace except that he periodically withdraw from the outer world of perishable things and reach inwardly towards the abiding and imperishable realities.

True Solitude Does Away With Religion

The consolations of the creeds are derived from the solitude which those creeds enforce. The regular observance of the ceremonies of formal religion, attended, as they are, with concentrated silence and freedom from worldly distractions, compels men to do unconsciously that which they have not yet learned to do consciously—namely, to concentrate the mind periodically on the inward silence, and meditate, though very briefly, on high and holy things.

The man who has not learned to control and purify his mind in seasons of chosen solitude, yet whose awakening aspirations grope for something higher and nobler than he yet possesses, feels the necessity for the aid of ceremonial religion. But he who has taken himself in hand with a view to self-conquest, who withdraws into solitude in order to grapple with his lower nature, and masterfully bend his mind in holy directions, requires no further aid from book or priest or Church. The Church does not exist for the pleasure of the saint but for the elevation of the sinner.

No Growth Without Solitude

In solitude a man gathers strength to meet the difficulties and temptations of life, knowledge to understand and conquer them, and wisdom to transcend them. As a building is preserved and sustained by virtue of the foundation which is hidden and unobserved, so a man is maintained perpetually in strength and peace by virtue of his lonely hour of intense thought which no eye beholds.

It is in solitude only that a man can be truly revealed to himself, that he can come to understand his real nature, with all its powers and possibilities. The voice of the spirit is not heard in the hubbub of the world and amid the clamors of conflicting desires. There can be no spiritual growth without solitude.

There are those who shrink from too close a scrutiny of themselves. They dread too complete a self-revelation, and fear that solitude which would leave them alone with their own thoughts and call up before their mental vision the ghost of their desires. And so they go where the chaos of pleasure is loudest and where the reproving voice of Truth is drowned.

But he who loves Truth, who desires and seeks wisdom, will be much alone. He will seek the fullest, clearest revelation of himself. He will avoid the haunts of frivolity and noise, and will go where the sweet, tender voice of the spirit of Truth speaks within him and can be heard.

The Fate of The Pleasure Seeker

Men go after much company and seek out new excitements, but they are not acquainted with peace. In diverse paths of pleasure they search for happiness but they do not come to rest. Through diverse ways of laughter and feverish delirium they wander after happiness and life, but their tears are many and grievous, and they do not escape death.

Drifting upon the ocean of life in search of selfish indulgences men are caught in its storms, and only after many tempests and much privation do they fly to the Rock of Refuge which rests in the deep silence of their own being.

While a man is absorbed in outward activities he is giving out his energies and becoming spiritually weaker. In order to retain his moral vigor he must resort to solitary meditation.

So needful is this that he who neglects it loses or does not attain the right knowledge of life. Nor does he comprehend and overcome those most deeply rooted and subtlest of sins which appear like virtues, deceiving the elect, and to which all but the truly wise succumb.

> *"True dignity abides with him alone,*
> *Who, in the silent hour of inward thought,*
> *Can still suspect and still revere himself*
> *In lowliness of heart."*

He who lives, without ceasing in outward excitement lives most in disappointments and griefs. Where the sounds of pleasure are greatest heart-emptiness is the keenest and deepest.

He, also, whose whole life, even if not one of lust for pleasure, is centered in outward works, who deals only with the changing panorama of visible things, never falling back in solitude upon the inner and invisible world of permanent being, such a man does not attain knowledge and wisdom, but remains empty. He cannot aid the world, cannot feed its aspirations, for he has no food to offer it, his spiritual store being empty.

The Wise Pursue Solitude

But he who courts solitude in order to search for the truth of things, who subdues his senses and makes quiet his desires, such a man is daily attaining knowledge and wisdom. He becomes filled with the spirit of truth. He can aid the world, for his spiritual store is full, and is kept well replenished.

While a man is absorbed in the contemplation of inward realities he is receiving knowledge and power. He opens himself, like a flower, to the universal light of Truth, and receives and drinks in its life-imparting rays. He also goes to the eternal foundation of knowledge and quenches his thirst in its inspiring waters. Such a man gains, in one hour of concentrated thought, more essential knowledge than a whole year's reading could impart.

Being is infinite and knowledge is illimitable and its source inexhaustible. He who draws upon the innermost depths of his being drinks from the spring of divine wisdom which can never run dry, and quaffs the waters of immortality.

Solitude Inspires Genius

It is this habitual association with the deep realities of Being, this continual drinking in of the Water of Life at its perennial source, that constitutes genius. The resources of genius are inexhaustible because they are drawn from the original and universal source, and for the same reason the works of genius are ever new and fresh. The more a genius gives out the fuller he becomes. With the accomplishment of every work his mind extends and expands, reaches out more vastly, and sees wider and ever wider ranges of power.

The genius is inspired. He has bridged the gulf between the finite and infinite. He needs no secondary aids, but draws from that universal spring which is the source of every noble work. The difference between an ordinary man and a genius is this—the one lives in outward appearances, the other in inward realities; the one goes after pleasure, the other after wisdom; the one relies on books, the other relies upon his own being.

Books Are Not The Source of Wisdom

Book-learning is good when its true place is understood, but it is not the source of wisdom. The source of wisdom is in life itself, and is comprehended by effort, practice, and experience. Books give information but they cannot bestow knowledge. They can stimulate but cannot accomplish—you must put forth effort, and achieve for yourself.

The man who relies entirely upon books, and does not go to the silent resources within, is superficial and becomes rapidly exhausted. He is uninspired (though he may be extremely clever), for he soon reaches the end of his stock of information, and so becomes void and repetitious. His work lacks the sweet spontaneity of life and ever-renewed freshness of inspiration. Such a man has cut himself off from the infinite supply and deals, not with life itself, but with dead or decaying appearances. Information is limited; the knowledge gained in solitude is boundless.

Genius Grows in Solitude

The inspiration of genius and greatness is fostered, evolved, and finally completed in solitude. The most ordinary man, who conceives a noble purpose, and, then summoning up all his energies and will, focuses upon and ripens his purpose in solitude, will, in time, accomplish his objective and become a genius.

The man who renounces the pleasures of the world, who avoids popularity and fame, and who works in obscurity and thinks in solitude for the accomplishment of a lofty ideal for the human race, becomes a seer and a prophet.

He who silently sweetens his heart, who attunes his mind to that which is pure, beautiful, and good, who in long hours of lonely contemplation strives to reach to the central and eternal heart of things, brings himself in touch with the inaudible harmonies of being. He opens himself for the reception of the cosmic song, and becomes at last a singer and a poet.

And so with all genius: it is the child of solitude—a very simple-hearted child—wide-eyed, listening, and beautiful, yet to the noise-enamored world, it seems an incomprehensible mystery, of which it is only now and then granted a glimpse from beyond the well-guarded Gates of Silence.

> *"In man's self arise*
> *August anticipations, symbols, types*
> *Of a dim splendor ever on before*
> *In that eternal circle life pursues."*

The Solitude of The Masters

Paul of Tarsus, the cruel persecutor and blind bigot, after spending three years alone in the desert, comes forth a loving apostle and an inspired seer.

Gautama Siddhartha, the man of the world, after six years (in the forest) of lonely struggle with his passions and intense meditation upon the deep mysteries of his nature, becomes Buddha, the enlightened one, the embodiment of calm, serene wisdom, to whom a heart-thirsty world turns to receive refreshing waters of immortality.

Lao-Tze, an ordinary citizen filling a worldly office, in his search for knowledge courts solitude, and discovers Tao, the Supreme Reason, by virtue of which he becomes a world-teacher.

Jesus, the unlettered carpenter, after many years of solitary communion upon the mountains with the Unfailing Love and Wisdom, comes forth a blessed savior of humankind.

Even after they had attained, and had scaled the lofty heights of divine knowledge these Great Souls were much alone, and retired frequently for brief seasons of solitude.

The greatest man will fall from his moral height and lose his influence if he neglects that renewal of power which can only be obtained in solitude. These Masters attained their power by consciously harmonizing their thoughts and lives with the creative energies within themselves. By transcending individuality and sinking their petty personal will in the Universal Will, they became Masters of Creative Thought, and stand as the loftiest instruments for the outworking of cosmic evolution.

Your True Home Is in Silence

Genius is not miraculous, it is a matter of law. It is not mysterious except in so far as law is mysterious. Every man becomes a creative master in so far as he subordinates himself to the universally good and true. Every poet, painter, saint, and sage is the mouthpiece of the Eternal. The perfection of the message varies with the measure of individual selflessness. In so far as self intervenes the distinctness of the work and message becomes blurred. Perfect selflessness is the acme of genius, the consummation of power.

Such self-surrender can only be begun, pursued, and completed in solitude. A man cannot gather together and concentrate his spiritual forces while he is engaged in spending those forces in worldly activities. Although the balance of forces can be maintained under all circumstances after power is attained, even in the midst of the antagonistic throng, spiritual power is only secured after many years of frequent and habitual solitude.

Man's true Home is in the Great Silence—this is the source of all that is real and abiding within. His present nature, however, is dual, and outer activities are necessary. Neither entire solitude nor entire action is the true life in the world. But that is the true life which gathers, in solitude, strength and wisdom to rightly perform the activities of life.

As a man returns to his home in the evening, weary with labor, for that sweet rest and refreshment which will prepare him for another day's toil, so must he, who would not break down in the labor of life, come away from the noise and toil of the world's great workshop and rest for brief periods in his abiding Home in the Silence. He who does this, spending some portion of each day in sacred and purposeful solitude, will become strong, useful, and blessed.

Solitude is for the strong, or for those who are ready to become strong. When a man is becoming great he becomes solitary. He goes in solitude to seek, and that which he seeks he finds, for there is a Way to all knowledge, all wisdom, all truth, and all power. The Way is forever open, but it lies through soundless solitudes and the unexplored silences of a man's being.

Standing Alone

IN THE LIFE OF BLESSEDNESS self-reliance is of the utmost importance. If there is to be peace there must be strength. If there is to be security there must be stability. If there is to be lasting joy there must be no leaning upon things which at any moment may be snatched away forever.

A man does not begin to truly live until he finds an immovable center within himself on which to stand, by which to regulate his life, and from which to draw his peace. If he trusts to that which fluctuates he also will fluctuate. If he leans upon that which may be withdrawn he will fall and be bruised. If he looks for satisfaction in perishable accumulations he will starve for happiness in the midst of plenty.

Let a man learn to stand alone, looking to no one for support; expecting no favors, craving no personal advantages; not begging nor complaining, not craving nor regretting, but relying upon the truth within himself. Let him derive his satisfaction and comfort from the integrity of his own heart.

If a man can find no peace within himself where shall he find it? If he dreads to be alone with himself what steadfastness shall he find in company? If he can find no joy in communion with his own thoughts, how shall he escape misery in his contact with others? The man who has yet found nothing within himself upon which to stand, will nowhere find a place of constant rest.

Happiness Rests Within, Not Without

Men everywhere are deluded by the superstition that their happiness rests with other people and with outward things, and, as a result, they live in continual disappointments, regrets, and lamentations.

The man who does not look for happiness from any others or from external things, but finds within himself the inexhaustible source, will be self-contained and serene under all circumstances. He will never become the helpless victim of misery and grief.

The man who looks to others for support, who measures his happiness by the conduct of others and not by his own, who depends upon their cooperation for his peace of mind—such a man has no spiritual foothold. His mind is tossed hither and thither with the continual changes going on around him, and he lives in that ceaseless ebb and flow of the spirits which is wretchedness and unrest. He is a spiritual cripple, and has yet to learn how to maintain his mental center of gravity, and so go without the aid of crutches.

Be Master of Your Own Kingdom

As a child learns to walk in order to go about from place to place by himself strong and unaided, so should a man learn to stand alone, to judge and think and act for himself, and to choose, in the strength of his own mind, the pathway which he shall walk.

Without is change, decay, and insecurity, within is all surety and blessedness. The soul is sufficient of itself. Where the need is there is the abundant supply. Your eternal dwelling-place is within. Go there and take possession of your mansion; there you are a king, elsewhere you are a servant.

Be contented that others shall manage or mismanage their own little kingdom, and see to it that you reign strongly over your own. Your entire well-being and the well-being of the whole world lies there. You have a conscience, follow it. You have a mind, clarify it. You have a judgement, use and improve it.

You have a will, employ and strengthen it. You have knowledge, increase it.

There is a light within your own soul; watch it, tend it, encourage it, shield it from the winds of passion, and help it to burn with a steadier and ever steadier radiance. Leave the world and come back to yourself. Be rich in yourself, be complete in yourself.

Find the abiding center within you and obey it. The earth is maintained in its orbit by its obedience to its center, the sun. Obey the center of light that is within you; let others call it darkness if they will. You are responsible for yourself, are accountable to yourself, therefore rely upon yourself.

If you fear yourself who will place confidence in you? If you are untrue to yourself where shall you find the sweet satisfaction of Truth?

Mistaking Pride for Self-Reliance

The great man stands alone in the simple dignity of independence. He pursues his own path fearlessly, and does not apologize or "beg leave." Criticism and applause are no more to him than the dust upon his coat, of which he shakes himself free. He is not guided by the changing opinions of others but guides himself by the light of his own mind. Other men barter away their freedom for portions of flattery or fashion.

Until you can stand alone, looking neither to spirits nor mortals, gods nor men, for guidance, but guiding yourself by the light of the truth within you, you are not unfettered and free, not altogether blessed.

But do not mistake pride for self-reliance. To attempt to stand upon the crumbling foundation of pride is to be already fallen. No man depends upon others more than the proud man. He drinks in their praise and resents their censure. He mistakes flattery for sound judgement, and is most easily hurt or pleased by the opinions of others. His happiness is entirely in the hands of others.

The self-reliant man stands, not upon his personal pride, but on an abiding law, principle, ideal, or reality within himself. Upon this he poises himself, refusing to be swept from his strong foothold either by the waves of passion within or the storms of opinion without. Should he at any time lose this balance he quickly regains himself, and is fully restored. His happiness is entirely in his own hands.

Learn From Everyone
Find your center of balance and succeed in standing alone, and, whatever your work in life may be, you

will succeed. You will accomplish what you set your mind upon, for the truly self-reliant are invincible.

But though you do not rely upon others, learn from them. Never cease to increase in knowledge, and be ever ready to receive that which is good and useful. You cannot not have too much humility. The most self-reliant men are the most humble.

"No aristocrat, no prince born to the purple, can begin to compare with the self-respect of the saint. Why is he lowly, but that he knows that he can well afford it, resting on the largeness of God in him."

Learn from all men, and especially from the masters of Truth, but do not lose your hold upon the truth that the ultimate guidance is in yourself. A master can say: "Here is the path," but he can neither compel you to walk it nor walk it for you. You must put forth your own efforts, must achieve by your own strength, must make his truth your truth by your own unaided exertions. You must implicitly trust yourself.

*"This thing is God—to be man with thy might,
To grow great in the strength of thy spirit,
And live out thy life as the light."*

Stand Alone With The Whole

You are to be master of yourself, lord over yourself, not fawning and imitating, but doing your work as a living, vital portion of the universe. Giving love but not expecting it; giving sympathy but not craving for it; giving aid but not depending upon it. If others should censure your work, heed them not. It suffices that your work be true: and rest in this sufficiency. Do not ask: "Will my work please?" but: "Is it real?" If your work be true the criticism of men cannot touch it. If it be false their disapproval will not slay it quicker than it will die of itself.

The words and acts of Truth cannot pass away until their work is fully accomplished. The words and acts of error cannot remain, for they have no work to do. Criticism and resentment alike are superfluous.

Free yourself from the self-imposed tyranny of slavish dependence, and stand alone, not as an isolated unit, but as a sympathetic portion of the whole. Find the Joy that results from well-earned freedom, the peace that flows from wise self-possession, the blessedness that inheres in native strength.

~ Byways of Blessedness

*"Honor to him who, self-complete, if lone,
Carves to the grave one pathway all his own,
And heeding naught that men may think or say,
Asks but his soul if doubtful of the way."*

*"By all means use to be alone,
Salute thyself; See what thy soul doth wear."*
—George Herbert

*"He that has light within his own clear breast
May sit in the center and enjoy bright day."*
—Milton

Understanding The Simple Laws of Life

WALKING THOSE BYWAYS which I have so far pointed out, resting in their beauty and drinking in their blessedness, the pilgrim along life's broad highway will, in due time, come to one wherein his last burden will fall from him. This is where all his weariness will pass away, where he will drink of light-hearted liberty, and rest in perpetual peace. And this most blessed of spiritual byways, the richest source of strength and comfort, I call *The Right Understanding of the Simple Laws of Life*.

He who comes to it leaves behind him all lack and longing, all doubt and perplexity, all sorrow and uncertainty. He lives in the fullness of satisfaction, in light and knowledge, in gladness and surety. He who comprehends the utter simplicity of life; who obeys its laws and does not step aside into the dark paths and complex mazes of selfish desire, stands where no harm can reach him. He stands where no enemy can lay him low—and doubts, desires, and sorrows are no more. Doubt ends where reality begins. Painful desire ceases where the fullness of joy is perpetual and complete. And when the Unfailing and Eternal Good is realized what room is there for sorrow?

Life Is Simple; We Make it Complex

Human life when rightly lived is simple with a beautiful simplicity. But it is not rightly lived while it is bound to a complexity of lusts, desires, and wants. These are not the real life but the burning fever and painful disease which originate in an unenlightened condition of mind. The curtailing of one's desires is the beginning of wisdom; their entire mastery its consummation. This is so because life is bounded by law, and, being inseparable from law, life has no need that is not already supplied. Now lust, or desire, is not need, but a rebellious superfluity, and as such it leads to deprivation and misery.

The prodigal son, while in his Father's house, not only had all that he required, but was surrounded by a superabundance. Desire was not necessary, because all things were at hand. But when desire entered his heart he "went into a far country," and "began to be in want," and it was only when he became reduced to the utmost extremity of starvation that he turned with longing towards his Father's Home.

This parable is symbolical of the evolution of the individual and the race. Man has come into such a complexity of cravings that he lives in continual discontent, dissatisfaction, want, and pain. His only cure lies in a return to the Father's Home—that is, to actual living or being as distinguished from desiring.

But a man does not do this until he is reduced to the last extremity of spiritual starvation. He has then reaped the experience of pain and sorrow as the result of desire. He looks back with longing towards the true life of peace and plenty. And so he turns around, and begins the toilsome journey back towards his Home, towards that rich life of simple being which is emancipation from the bondage, fever, and hunger of desire. This longing for the true life, for Truth and Reality, should not be confounded with desire: it is aspiration.

Desire Can Never Be Satisfied

Desire is the craving for possession; aspiration is the hunger of the heart for peace. The craving for things leads ever farther and farther from peace. It not only ends in deprivation but is, in itself, a state of perpetual want. Until desire comes to an end, rest and satisfaction is an impossibility.

The hunger for things can never be satisfied, but the hunger for peace can, and the satisfaction of peace is found, is fully possessed, when all selfish desire is abandoned. Then there is fullness of joy, abounding plenty, and rich and complete blessedness. In this supremely blessed state, life is comprehended in its perfect symmetry and simplicity, and the acme of power and usefulness is attained. Then even the hunger for peace ceases, for peace becomes the normal condition, is fully possessed, constant, and never-varying.

Men, immersed in desire, ignorantly imagine that the conquest of desire leads to inactivity, loss of power, and lifelessness. Instead, it leads to highly concentrated activity, to the full employment of power, and to a life so rich, so glorious, and so abundantly blessed as to be incomprehensible to those who hunger for pleasures and possessions. Of this life only can it be said:

*"Here are no sounds of discord—no profane
Or senseless gossip of unworthy things—*

Only the songs of chisels and of pens,
Of busy brushes, and ecstatic strains
Of souls surcharged with music most divine.
Here is no idle sorrow, no poor grief
For any day or object left behind—
For time is counted precious, and herein
Is such complete abandonment of Self
That tears turn into rainbows, and enhance
The beauty of the land where all is fair."

The Enlightened Have No Desire

When a man is rescued from selfish desire his mind is unencumbered, and he is free to work for humanity. No longer racing after those gratifications which leave him hungry still, all his powers are at his immediate command. Seeking no rewards he can concentrate all his energies upon the faultless completion of his duties, and so accomplish all things and fulfill all righteousness.

The fully enlightened and fully blessed man is not prompted to action by desire but works from knowledge. The man of desire needs the promise of a reward to urge him to action. He is as a child working for the possession of a toy. But the man of knowledge, living in the fullness of life and power, can at any moment bring his energies into requisition for the accomplishment of that which is necessary. He is, spiritually, a full-grown man. For him all rewards have ceased; to him all occurrences are good. He lives always in complete satisfaction. Such a man has attained to life, and his delight (and it is a sweet, perpetual, and never-failing delight) is in obedience to the simple demands of exact and never-failing law.

But this life of supreme blessedness is an end, and the pilgrim who is striving towards it, the prodigal returning to it, must travel to that end, and employ means to get there. He must pass through the country of his animal desires, disentangling himself from their intricacies, simplifying them, and overcoming them. This is the way, and he has no enemies but what spring forth within himself.

At first the way seems hard because, blinded by desire, he does not perceive the simple structure of life, and its laws are hidden from him. But as he becomes more simple in his mind, the direct laws of life become unfolded to his spiritual perception, and at once the point is reached where these laws begin to be understood and obeyed. Then the way becomes plain and easy. There is no more uncertainty and darkness, but all is seen in the clear light of knowledge.

It will help to accelerate the progress of the searcher for the true and blessed life if we now turn to a consideration of some of these simple laws which are rigidly mathematical in their operations.

"The elementary laws never apologize."

The Law of Oneness

All life is one, though it has a diversity of manifestations. All law is one, but it is applicable and operative in a variety of ways. There is not one law for matter and another for mind, not one for the material and visible and another for the spiritual and invisible. There is the same law throughout.

There is not one kind of logic for the world and another for the spirit, but the same logic is applicable to both. Men faithfully, and with unerring worldly wisdom, observe certain laws or rules of action in material things. They know that to ignore or disobey them would be great folly on their part, ending in disaster for themselves and confusion for society and the state. But they err in supposing and believing that the same rules do not apply in spiritual things, and thereby suffer for their ignorance and disobedience.

~ Byways of Blessedness

Most People Are Spiritual Beggars

It is a law in worldly things that a man shall support himself, that he shall earn his living, and that "He that will not work, neither shall he eat." Men observe this law, recognizing its justice and goodness, and so earn the necessary material sustenance.

But in spiritual things men, broadly speaking, deny and ignore the operation of this law. They think that it is absolutely just that a man should earn his material bread, and that the man who shirks this law should wander in rags and want. Yet, they think it is right that they should beg for their spiritual bread, and just that they should receive all spiritual blessings without either deserving or attempting to earn them.

The result is that most people wander in spiritual beggary and want—that is, in suffering and sorrow—deprived of spiritual sustenance, of joy, knowledge and peace.

Worldly Versus Spiritual Law

If you are in need of any worldly thing—food, clothing, furniture, or other necessity—you do not beg of the storekeeper to give it to you. You ask the price of it, pay for it with your money, and then it becomes your own. You recognize the perfect justice

The Wisdom of James Allen III ~

in giving an equivalent for what you receive, and would not wish it to be otherwise.

The same just law prevails in spiritual things. If you are in need of any spiritual thing—joy, assurance, peace, or whatsoever—you can only come into full possession of it by giving an equivalent. You must pay the price for it. As you must give a portion of your material substance for a worldly thing so you must give a portion of your immaterial substance for a spiritual thing. You must yield up some passion, lust, vanity or indulgence before the spiritual possession can be yours.

The miser who clings to his money and will not give up any of it because of the pleasure which its possession affords him cannot have any of the material comforts of life. He lives in continual want and discomfort in spite of all his wealth.

The man who will not give up his passions, who clings to anger, unkindness, sensuality, pride, vanity, self-indulgence, for the momentary pleasure which their gratification affords him is a spiritual miser. He cannot have any spiritual comforts, and suffers continual spiritual want and uneasiness in spite of the wealth of worldly pleasures which he fondly hugs and refuses to give up.

The man who is wise in worldly things neither

begs nor steals, but labors and purchases, and the world honors him for his uprightness.

The man who is wise in spiritual things neither begs nor steals, but labors in his own inner world, and purchases his spiritual possessions. And the whole universe honors him for his righteousness.

Wanting Something for Nothing

It is another law in worldly things that a man who engages himself to another in any form of employment shall be content with the wages upon which he agreed. If at the end of his week's work, and on receiving his wages, he were to ask his employer for a larger sum, pleading that, though he could not justly claim it and did not really deserve it, he yet expected it, he would not only not receive the larger sum but would, doubtless, be discharged from his post.

Yet in spiritual things men do not think it to be either foolish or selfish to ask for those blessings—spiritual wages—upon which they never agreed, for which they never labored, and which they do not deserve. Every man gets from the law of the universe that upon which he agrees and for which he works—no more, no less; and he is continually entering into agreements with the Supreme Law—the Master of the universe. For every thought and act which he gives he receives its just equivalent. For all work done in the form of deeds he receives the wages due to him.

Knowing this, the enlightened man is always content, always satisfied, and in perfect peace, knowing that whatever he receives (be it called misfortune or good fortune) he has earned. The Great Law never cheats any man of his just due, but it says to the complainer and the griper, "Friend, did you not agree with me for a penny a day?"

Accumulating Spiritual Wealth

Again, if a man would grow rich in worldly goods he must economize, and manage his financial resources until he has accumulated sufficient capital to invest in some branch of industry. Then he must judiciously invest his little store of capital, neither holding it too tightly nor letting it go carelessly. He thus increases both in worldly wisdom and worldly riches. The idle spendthrift cannot grow rich. He is wasteful and riotous.

He who would grow rich in spiritual things must also economize, and direct his mental resources. He must curb his tongue and impulses, not wasting his energy in idle gossip, vain argument, or excesses of temper. In this way he will accumulate a little store of wisdom which is his spiritual capital. And this he must send out into the world for the good of others. The more he uses it the richer will he become.

Thus does a man increase in both heavenly wisdom and heavenly riches. The man who follows blind impulses and desires and does not control and govern this mind is a spiritual spendthrift. He can never become rich in divine things.

Effort Is Required in All Undertakings

It is a physical law that if we would reach the summit of a mountain we must climb in that direction. The path must be sought and then carefully followed. And the climber must not give up and go back because of the labor involved and the difficulties to be overcome, nor on account of aching limbs, otherwise the summit cannot be reached. This law is also spiritual.

He who would reach the high altitudes of moral or intellectual grandeur must climb in that direction by his own efforts. He must seek out the pathway and then assiduously follow it, not giving up and turning back, but by surmounting all difficulties, and enduring for a time trials, temptations, and heartaches. Then, at last he will stand upon the glorious summit of moral perfection, with the world of passion, temptation, and sorrow beneath his feet, and the boundless heavens of dignity stretching vast and silent above his head.

If a man would reach a distant city, or any place of destination, he must travel in that direction. There is no law by which he can be instantly transported there. He can only get there by putting forth the necessary exertion. If he walks he will put forth great exertion, but it will cost him nothing in money. If he drives or takes a train, there will be less actual labor, but he must pay in money for that which he has labored. To reach any place requires labor. This cannot be avoided; it is law.

It is equally so spiritually. He who would reach any spiritual destination, such as purity, compassion, wisdom, or peace, must travel in that direction, and must labor to get there. There is no law by which he can suddenly be transported to any of these beautiful spiritual cities. He must find the most direct route and then put forth the necessary effort. Then, at last he will come to the end of his journey.

The Universe Has No Favorites

These are but a few of the many laws, or manifestations of the One Great Law, which are to be understood, applied, and obeyed before the full maturity of spiritual life and blessedness can be attained. There is no worldly or physical law which does not operate, with equal exactness, in the spiritual realm—that is, the inner and invisible world of man's being.

Just as physical things are the shadows and types of spiritual realities, so worldly wisdom is the reflected image of Divine Wisdom. All those simple operations of human life in worldly things which men never question, but follow and obey implicitly because of their obvious plainness and exactness, succeed in spiritual things with the same unerring accuracy.

When this is understood, and these laws are as implicitly obeyed in spiritual as in worldly matters, then a man will have reached the firm ground of exact knowledge. His sorrows are at an end, and he can doubt no more.

Everything Happens for The Best

Life is uninvolved, uncompromising justice. Its operations are simple, invincible logic. Law reigns forever, and the heart of law is love. Favoritism and caprice are the reverse of both law and love. The universe has no favorites; it is supremely just, and gives to every person his or her rightful earnings. All is good because all is according to law. And because all is according to law, man can find the right way in life, and, having found it, can rejoice and be glad.

The Father of Jesus is the Unfailing Good which is embodied in the law of things. "No evil can happen to a good man either in life or death." Jesus recognized the good in his own fate, and exonerated all his persecutors from blame. "No man," he declared, "taketh my life from me, but I lay it down of myself." That is, he himself had brought about his own end.

He who has simplified his life and purified his mind, will arrive at an understanding of the beautiful simplicity of being. He will perceive the unvarying operation of law in all things. He knows the results of all his thoughts and deeds upon himself and the world. He knows what effects are bound up with the mental causes which he sets in motion.

He will then think and do only those thoughts and deeds that are blessed in their inception, blessed in their growth, and blessed in their completion. Humbly accepting the lawful results of all the deeds done when in a state of ignorance, he will neither complain, nor fear, nor question. He will be at rest in obedience, perfectly blessed in his knowledge of the Good Law.

~ Byways of Blessedness

"*The tissue of our life to be
We weave with colors all our own,
And in the field of Destiny
We reap as we have sown.*

"*And if we reap as we have sown,
And take the dole we deal,
The law of pain is love alone,
The wounding is to heal.*"

"*Watch narrowly
The demonstration of a truth, its birth,
And you trace back the effluence to its spring
And source within us.*"
—*Browning*

"*More is the treasure of the Law than gems;
Sweeter than comb its sweetness. It delights,
Delightful past compare.*"
—*The Light of Asia*

Happy Endings

LIFE HAS MANY happy endings, because it has much that is noble, pure, and beautiful. Although there is much sin and ignorance in the world, many tears, and much pain and sorrow, there is also much purity and knowledge, many smiles, and much healing and gladness. No pure thought, no unselfish deed can fall short of its happy result, and every such result is a happy end point.

A pleasant home is a happy ending. A successful life is a happy ending. A task well and faithfully done is a happy ending. To be surrounded by kind friends is a happy ending. A quarrel put away, grudges wiped out, unkind words confessed and forgiven, friend restored to friend—all these are happy endings. To find that which one has long and tediously sought; to be restored from tears to gladness; to awaken in the bright sunlight out of the painful nightmare of sin; to attain, after much searching, the Heavenly Way in life—these are, indeed, blessed end points.

He who looks for, finds, and enters the byways which I have indicated will come to this without seeking it, for his whole life will be filled with happy endings. He who begins right and continues right does not need to desire and search for happy results. They are already at hand. They follow as consequences. They are the certainties, the realities of life.

There are happy endings which belong solely to the material world. These are transient, and they pass away. There are happy endings which belong to the spiritual world. These are eternal, and they do not pass away. Sweet are companionships, pleasures, and material comforts, but they change and fade away. Sweeter still are Purity, Wisdom, and the knowledge of Truth, and these never change nor fade away.

Freeing Your Heart From Worldly Desire

Wherever a man goes in this world he can take his worldly possessions with him. But soon he must part company with them, and if he stands upon these alone, deriving all his happiness from them, he will come to a spiritual ending of great emptiness and want. But he who has attained to the possession of spiritual things can never be deprived of his source of happiness. He will never have to part company with it. And wherever he goes in the whole universe he will carry his possessions with him. His spiritual end will be the fullness of joy.

Happy in the Eternal Happiness is he who has come to that Life from which the thought of self is abolished. Already, even now and in this life, he has entered the Kingdom of Heaven, Nirvana, Paradise, the New Jerusalem, the Olympus of Jupiter, the Valhalla of the Gods. He knows the Final Unity of Life, the Great Reality of which these fleeting and changing names are but feeble utterances. He is at rest on the bosom of the Infinite.

Sweet is the rest and deep the bliss of him who has freed his heart from its lusts, hatreds, and dark desires. When man is without any shadow of bitterness or selfishness, he can look out upon the world with boundless compassion and love, and breathe, in his inmost heart, the blessing: *Peace unto all living things*.

Such a man makes no exceptions or distinctions—he has reached that happy ending which can never be taken away, for this is the perfection of life, the fullness of peace, the consummation of perfect blessedness.

> *"Such is the Law which moves to righteousness,*
> *Which none at last can turn aside or stay;*
> *The heart of it is Love, the end of it*
> *Is peace and consummation sweet. Obey."*
> —The Light of Asia

> *"So, haply, when thy task shall end,*
> *The wrong shall lose itself in right,*
> *And all thy week-day Sabbaths blend*
> *With the long Sabbath of the Light!"*
> —Whittier

Amid the din and strife of men,
The Call Divine I hear again;
Its telling is of things apart;
Above the tumult of the heart.
High o'er where sin's dark pathways wind
Waits the wise willing of the mind;
Beyond strong Passion's guarded Gates,
There Peace awaits—there Peace awaits.

Book THREE

From Passion to Peace

From Passion to Peace

Table of Contents

Foreword..251

Passion..252

Aspiration...258

Temptation...264

Transmutation..270

Transcendence.......................................277

Beatitude...286

Peace...291

Foreword

THE FIRST THREE PARTS of this book, *Passion*, *Aspiration*, and *Temptation*, represent the common human life, with its passion, pathos, and tragedy. The last three parts, *Transcendence*, *Beatitude*, and *Peace*, represents the Divine Life—calm, wise and beautiful—of the sage and Savior. The middle part, *Transmutation*, is the transitional stage between the two; it is the alchemic process linking the divine with the human life. Discipline, denial, and renunciation do not constitute the Divine State; they are only the means by which it is attained. The Divine Life is established in that Perfect Knowledge which bestows Perfect Peace.

—*James Allen*

Passion

THE PATHWAY OF THE SAINTS and sages, the road of the wise and the pure; the highway along which the Saviors have trod, and which all Saviors to come will also walk—such is the subject of this book; such is the high and holy theme which the author briefly expounds in these pages.

Passion is the lowest level of human life. None can descend lower. In its chilling swamps and concealing darkness creep and crawl the creatures of the sunless world. Lust, hatred, anger, covetousness, pride, vanity, greed, revenge, envy, backbiting, lying, theft, deceit, treachery, cruelty, suspicion, jealousy—such are the brute forces and blind, unreasoning impulses that inhabit the underworld of passion, and roam, devouring and devoured, in the rank primeval jungles of the human mind.

There also dwell the dark shapes of remorse, pain,

and suffering, and the drooping forms of grief, sorrow, and lamentation.

In this dark world the unwise live and die, not knowing the peace of purity, nor the joy of that Divine Light which forever shines above them, and for them. Yet, it shines in vain so long as it falls on unseeing eyes which look not up, but are ever bent earthward—fleshward.

But the wise look up. They are not satisfied with this passion-world. They bend their steps towards the upper world of peace, the light and the glory of which they behold, at first far off, but nearer and with ever increasing splendor as they ascend.

None can fall lower than passion, but all can rise higher. In that lowest place where further descent is impossible, all who move forward must ascend. The ascending pathway is always at hand, near, and easily accessible. It is the way of self-conquest. He has already entered it who has begun to say "nay" to his selfishness, who has begun to discipline his desires, and to control and command the unruly elements of his mind.

Selfishness Is Born of Ignorance

Passion is the archenemy of mankind, the slayer of happiness, the opposite and enemy of peace. From it proceeds all that defiles and destroys. It is the source of misery, and the promulgator of mischief and disaster.

The inner world of selfishness is rooted in ignorance—ignorance of Divine Law, of Divine Goodness; ignorance of the Pure Way and the Peaceful Path. Passion is dark, and it thrives and flourishes in spiritual darkness. It cannot enter the regions of spiritual light. In the enlightened mind the darkness of ignorance is destroyed; in the pure heart there is no place for passion.

Passion in all its forms is a mental thirst, a fever, a torturing unrest. As a fire consumes a magnificent building, reducing it to a heap of unsightly ashes, so are men consumed by the flames of passions, and their deeds and works fall and perish.

If one would find peace, he must come out of passion. The wise man subdues his passions, the foolish man is subdued by them. The seeker for wisdom begins by turning his back on folly. The lover of peace enters the way which leads thereto, and with every step he takes he leaves further below and behind him the dark dwelling-place of passion and despair.

Understanding—The First Step
The first step towards the heights of wisdom and peace is to understand the darkness and misery of

~ From Passion to Peace

selfishness, and when that is understood, the overcoming of it—the coming out of it—will follow.

Selfishness, or passion, not only subsists in the gross forms of greed and glaringly ungoverned conditions of mind; it informs also every hidden thought which is subtly connected with the assumption and glorification of one's self. It is most deceiving and subtle when it prompts one to dwell upon the selfishness in others, to accuse them of it and to talk about it. The man who continually dwells upon the selfishness in others will not thus overcome his own selfishness. Not by accusing others do we come out of selfishness, but by purifying ourselves.

The way from passion to peace is not by hurling painful charges against others, but by overcoming one's self. By eagerly striving to subdue the selfishness of others, we remain passion-bound. By patiently overcoming our own selfishness, we ascend into freedom. Only he who has conquered himself can subdue others; and he subdues them, not by passion, but by love.

The foolish man accuses others and justifies himself; but he who is becoming wise justifies others and accuses himself. The way from passion to peace is not in the outer world of people; it is in the inner world of thoughts; it does not consist in altering the deeds of others, it consists in perfecting one's own deeds.

Frequently, the man of passion is most eager to put others right; but the man of wisdom puts himself right. If one is anxious to reform the world, let him begin by reforming himself. The reformation of self does not end with the elimination of the sensual elements only; that is its beginning. It ends only when every vain thought and selfish aim is overcome. Short of perfect purity and wisdom, there is still some form of self-slavery or folly which needs to be conquered.

Passion Is Foolish, Misdirected Power

Passion is at the base of the structure of life; peace is at its crown and summit. Without passion to begin with, there would be no power to work with, and no achievement to end with. Passion represents power, but power misdirected, power producing hurt instead of happiness. Its forces, while instruments of destruction in the hands of the foolish, are instruments of preservation in the hands of the wise. When curbed and concentrated and beneficially directed, they represent working energy. Passion is the flaming sword which guards the gates of Paradise. It shuts out and destroys the foolish; it admits and preserves the wise.

~ From Passion to Peace

He is the foolish man who does not know the extent of his own ignorance; who is the slave of thoughts of self; who obeys the impulses of passion. He is the wise man who knows his own ignorance; who understands the emptiness of selfish thoughts; who masters the impulses of passion.

The fool descends into deeper and deeper ignorance; the wise man ascends into higher and higher knowledge. The fool desires, suffers, and dies. The wise man aspires, rejoices, and lives.

With mind intent on wisdom and mental gaze raised upward, the spiritual warrior perceives the upward way, and fixes his attention upon the heights of Peace.

Aspiration

WITH THE CLEAR PERCEPTION of one's own ignorance comes the desire for enlightenment, and thus in the heart is born Aspiration, the rapture of the saints.

On the wings of aspiration man rises from earth to heaven, from ignorance to knowledge, from the under darkness to the upper light. Without it he remains a groveling animal, earthly, sensual, unenlightened, and uninspired.

Aspiration is the longing for heavenly things—for righteousness, compassion, purity, love—as distinguished from desire, which is the longing for earthly things—for selfish possessions, personal dominance, low pleasures, and sensual gratifications.

As a bird deprived of its wings cannot soar, so a man without aspiration cannot rise above his surroundings and become master of his animal inclinations. He is the slave of passions, is subject to others, and is carried hither and thither by the changing current of events.

For one to begin to aspire means that he is dissatisfied with his low status, and is aiming at a higher condition. It is a sure sign that he is aroused out of his lethargic sleep of animality, and has become conscious of nobler attainments and a fuller life.

Aspiration Unlocks The Gates to Everything

Aspiration makes all things possible. It opens the way to advancement. Even the highest state of perfection conceivable it brings near and makes real and possible; for that which can be conceived can be achieved.

Aspiration is the twin angel to inspiration. It unlocks the gates of joy. Singing accompanies soaring. Music, poetry, prophecy, and all high and holy instruments are at last placed in the hands of those whose aspirations flag not, whose spirit does not fail.

So long as animal conditions taste sweet to a man, he cannot aspire; he is already satisfied. But when their sweetness turns to bitterness, then in his sorrow he thinks of nobler things. When he is deprived of earthly joy, he aspires to the joy which is heavenly. It is when impurity turns to suffering that purity is sought. Truly aspiration rises, phoenix-like, from the dead ashes of repentance, but on its powerful pinions man can reach the heaven of heavens.

The man of aspiration has entered the way which ends in peace, and surely he will reach that end if he neither stays nor turns back. If he constantly renews his mind with glimpses of the heavenly vision, he will reach the heavenly state.

High and Low Aspiration

Man attains in the measure that he aspires. His longing to be is the gauge of what he can be. To fix the mind is to foreordain the achievement. As man can experience and know all low things, so he can experience and know all high things. As he has become human, so can he become divine. The turning of the mind in high and divine directions is the sole and needful task.

What is impurity but the impure thoughts of the thinker? What is purity but the pure thoughts of the thinker? One man does not do the thinking of another. Each man is pure or impure of himself alone.

If a man thinks, "It is through others, or circumstances, or heredity that I am impure," how can he

~ From Passion to Peace

hope to overcome his errors? Such a thought will check all holy aspirations and bind him to the slavery of passion.

When a man fully perceives that his errors and impurities are his own, that they are generated and fostered by himself, that he alone is responsible for them, then he will aspire to overcome them. The way of attainment will be opened up to him, and he will see from where and to what destination he is traveling.

The Pathways of Passion and Aspiration

The man of passion sees no straight path before him, and behind him is all fog and gloom. He seizes the pleasure of the moment and does not strive for understanding or think of wisdom. His way is confused, turbulent, and troubled, and his heart is far from peace.

The man of aspiration sees before him the pathway up the heavenly heights, and behind him are the circuitous routes of passion up which he has hitherto blindly groped. Striving for understanding, and his mind set on wisdom, his way is clear, and his heart already experiences a foretaste of the final peace.

Men of passion strive mightily to achieve little things—things which speedily perish, and, in the place where they were, leave nothing to be remembered.

Men of aspiration strive with equal might to achieve great things—things of virtue, of knowledge, of wisdom, which do not perish, but stand as monuments of inspiration for the uplifting of humankind.

As the merchant achieves worldly success by persistent exertion, so the saint achieves spiritual success by aspiration and endeavor. One becomes a merchant, the other a saint, by the particular direction in which his mental energy is guided.

Aspiration Is Strengthened Daily

When the rapture of aspiration touches the mind, it at once refines it, and the dross of its impurities begins to fall away. While aspiration holds the mind, no impurity can enter it, for the impure and the pure cannot at the same moment occupy the thought. But the effort of aspiration is at first spasmatic and short-lived. The mind falls back into its habitual error, and must be constantly renewed.

The lover of the pure life renews his mind daily with the invigorating glow of aspiration. He rises early, and fortifies his mind with strong thoughts and strenuous endeavor. He knows that the mind is of such a nature that it cannot remain for a moment unoccupied, and that if it is not held and guided by high thoughts and pure aspirations, it will assuredly be enslaved and misguided by low thoughts and base desires.

Aspiration can be fed, fostered, and strengthened by daily habit, just as is desire. It can be sought, and admitted into the mind as a divine guide, or it can be neglected and shut out. To retire for a short time each day to some quiet spot, preferably in the open air, and there call up the energies of the mind in surging waves of holy rapture, is to prepare the mind for great spiritual victories and destinies of divine import. For such a rapture is the preparation for wisdom and the prelude to peace.

Before the mind can contemplate pure things it must be lifted up to them, it must rise above impure things; and aspiration is the instrument by which this is accomplished. By its aid the mind soars swiftly and surely into heavenly places, and begins to experience divine things. It begins to accumulate wisdom, and to learn to guide itself by an ever-increasing measure of the divine light of pure knowledge.

To thirst for righteousness; to hunger for the pure life; to rise in holy rapture on the wings of angelic aspiration— this is the right road to wisdom. This is the right striving for peace. This is the right beginning of the way divine.

Temptation

ASPIRATION CAN CARRY a man into heaven, but to remain there, he must learn to conform his entire mind to the heavenly conditions. To this end temptation works.

Temptation is the reversion, in thought, from purity to passion. It is going back from aspiration to desire. It threatens aspiration until the point is reached where desire is quenched in the waters of pure knowledge and calm thought.

In the early stages of aspiration, temptation is subtle and powerful, and is regarded as an enemy; but it is only an enemy in the sense that the one tempted is his own enemy. In the sense that it is the revealer of weakness and impurity, it is a friend, a necessary factor in spiritual training. It is, indeed, an accompaniment of the effort to overcome evil and apprehend good. To be successfully conquered, the evil in a man must come to the surface and present itself, and it is in temptation that the evil hidden in the heart stands revealed and exposed.

Temptation Is Within, Not Without

That which temptation appeals to and arouses is unconquered desire, and temptation will again and again assail a man until he has lifted himself above the lusting impulses. Temptation is an appeal to the impure. That which is pure cannot be subject to temptation.

Temptation waylays the man of aspiration until he touches the region of the divine consciousness, and beyond that border temptation cannot follow him. It is when a man begins to aspire that he begins to be tempted. Aspiration rouses up all the latent good and evil, in order that the man may be fully revealed to himself, for a man cannot overcome himself unless he fully knows himself.

It can scarcely be said of the merely animal man that he is tempted, for the very presence of temptation means that there is a striving for a purer state. Animal desire and gratification is the normal condition of the man who has not yet risen into aspiration. He wishes for nothing more, nothing better, than his sensual enjoyments, and is, for the present, satisfied. Such a man cannot be tempted to fall, for he has not yet risen.

The presence of aspiration signifies that a man has taken one step, at least, upward, and is therefore capable of being drawn back. This backward attraction is called temptation. The allurements of temptation subsist in the impure thoughts and downward desires of the heart. The object of temptation is powerless to attract when the heart no longer lusts for it. The stronghold of temptation is within a man, not without; and until a man realizes this, the period of temptation will be prolonged.

While a man continues to run away from outward objects, under the delusion that temptation subsists entirely in them, and does not attack and purge away his impure imaginings, his temptations will increase, and his falls will be many and grievous. When a man clearly perceives that the evil is within and not without, then his progress will be rapid, his temptations will decrease, and the final overcoming of all temptation will be well within the range of his spiritual vision.

Temptation Must Be Understood

Temptation is torment. It is not an abiding condition, but is a passage from a lower condition to a higher. The fullness and perfection of life is bliss, not torment. Temptation accompanies weakness and defeat, but a man is destined for strength and victory. The presence of torment is the signal to rise and conquer. The man of persistent and ever renewed aspiration does not allow himself to think that temptation cannot be overcome. He is determined to be master of himself. Resignation to evil is an acknowledgement of defeat. It signifies that the battle against self is abandoned; that good is denied; that evil is made supreme.

As the energetic man of business is not daunted by difficulties but studies how to overcome them, so the man of ceaseless aspiration is not crushed into submission by temptations, but meditates how he may fortify his mind. For the tempter is like a coward: he only creeps in at weak and unguarded points.

The tempted one should study thoughtfully the nature and meaning of temptation, for until it is known it cannot be overcome. A wise general, before attacking the opposing force, studies the tactics of his enemy. Likewise, he who is to overcome temptation must understand how it arises in his own darkness and error, and must study, by introspection and meditation, how to disperse the darkness and supplant error by truth.

The stronger a man's passions, the fiercer will be his temptations; the deeper his selfishness, the more subtle his temptations; the more pronounced his vanity, the more flattering and deceptive his temptations.

You Must Study Your Weaknesses

A man must know himself if he is to know the truth. He must not shrink from any revelation which will expose his error. On the contrary, he must welcome such revelations as aids to that self-knowledge which is the handmaid of self-conquest.

The man who cannot endure to have his errors and shortcomings brought to the surface and made known, but tries to hide them, is unfit to walk the highway of truth. He is not properly equipped to battle with and overcome temptation. He who cannot fearlessly face his lower nature, cannot climb the rugged heights of renunciation.

Let the tempted one know this: that he himself is both tempter and tempted; that all his enemies are within; that the flatterers which seduce, the taunts which stab, and the flames which burn, all spring from that inner region of ignorance and error in which he has hitherto lived. Knowing this, let him be assured of complete victory over evil. When he is sorely tempted, let him not mourn, therefore, but let him rejoice in that his strength is tried and his weaknesses exposed. For he who truly knows and humbly acknowledges his weakness will not be slow in setting about the acquisition of strength.

The Foolish Lay Blame on Others

Foolish men blame others for their lapses and sins, but let the truth-lover blame only himself. Let him acknowledge his complete responsibility for his own conduct and not say, when he falls, this thing, or such and such a circumstance, or that man was to blame. For the most which others can do is to afford an opportunity for our own good or evil to manifest itself. They cannot make us good or evil.

Temptation is at first sore, grievous, and hard to be borne, and subtle and persistent is the assailant. But if the tempted one is firm and courageous, and does not give way, he will gradually subdue his spiritual enemy, and will finally triumph in the knowledge of good.

The adverse one is compounded of a man's own lust, selfishness, and pride. When these are put away, evil is seen to be naught, and good is revealed in all-victorious splendor.

Transmutation

MIDWAY BETWEEN the hell of Passion and the heaven of Peace is the purgatory of Transmutation—not a speculative purgatory beyond the grave, but a real purgatory in the human heart. In its separating and purifying fire the base metal of error is sifted away, and only the clarified gold of truth remains.

When temptation has culminated in sorrow and deep perplexity, then the tempted one, strenuously striving for deliverance, finds that his moral servitude is entirely from himself. Instead of fighting against outer circumstances, he must alter inner conditions. The fight against outer things is necessary at the start. It is the only course which can be adopted at the first, because of the prevailing ignorance of mental causation. But it never, of itself, brings about emancipation. What it does bring about is the knowledge of the mental cause of temptation. This knowledge of the mental cause of temptation leads to the transmutation of thought, and the transmutation of thought leads to deliverance from the bondage of error.

The preliminary fighting is a necessary stage in spiritual development, just as the crying and kicking of a helpless babe is necessary to its growth. But as the crying and kicking is not needed beyond the infant stage, so the fierce struggling with, and falling under, temptation ends when the knowledge of mental transmutation is acquired.

The Enlightened Do Not Struggle

The truly wise man, he who is enlightened concerning the source and cause of temptation, does not fight against outward allurements—he abandons all desire for them. Thus, they cease to be allurements, and the power of temptation is destroyed at its source. But this abandonment of unholy desire is not a final process. It is the beginning of a regenerative and transforming power which, when patiently employed, leads to the clear and cloudless heights of spiritual enlightenment.

Spiritual transmutation consists of an entire reversal of the ordinary self-seeking attitude of mind toward people and things, and this reversal brings about an entirely new set of experiences. Thus the desire for a certain pleasure is abandoned, cut off at its source, and not allowed to have any place in the consciousness. But the mental force which that desire represented is not annihilated, it is transferred to a higher region of thought, transmuted into a purer form of energy. The law of conservation of energy prevails universally in the mind as it does in matter, and the force shut off in lower directions is liberated in higher realms of spiritual activity.

Old Habits and Ways Are Abandoned

Along the Saintly Way towards the divine life, the midway region of Transmutation is the Country of Sacrifice, the Plain of Renunciation. Old passions, old ambitions and thoughts, are cast away and abandoned, but only to reappear in some more beautiful, more permanent, more eternally satisfying form.

Valuable jewels, long guarded and cherished, when thrown tearfully into the melting-pot, are remolded into new and more perfect adornments. Likewise, the spiritual alchemist, at first reluctant to part company with long-cherished thoughts and habits, at last gives them up to discover, a little later, to his joy, that they come back to him in the form of new facilities, rarer powers, and purer joys—spiritual jewels newly polished, beautiful, and resplendent.

The Process of Transmutation

In transmuting his mind from evil to good, a man comes to distinguish more and more clearly between error and Truth, and so distinguishing, he ceases to be swayed and prompted by outward things and by the actions and attitudes of others. Instead, he acts from his knowledge of truth. First acknowledging his errors, and then confronting them with a searching mind and a humble heart, he subdues, conquers, and transmutes them.

The early stage of transmutation is painful but brief, for the pain is soon transformed into pure spiritual joy, the brevity of the pain being measured by the intelligence and energy with which the process is pursued.

While a man thinks that the cause of his pain is in the attitude of others, he will not pass beyond it. But when he perceives that its cause is in himself, then he will pass beyond it into joy.

The unenlightened man allows himself to be disturbed, wounded, and overthrown by what he regards as the wrong attitude of others towards him. This is because the same wrong attitude is in himself. He, indeed, doles out to them, in return, the same actions, regarding as right in himself that which is wrong in others. Slander is given for slander, hatred for hatred, anger for anger. This is the action and reaction of evil. It is the clash of selfishness with selfishness. It is only the self, or selfish elements, within a man that can be aroused by the evil in another. The Truth, or divine characteristics, in a man cannot be approached by that evil, much less can it be disturbed and overthrown by it.

The Abandonment of Delusion

It is the conversion, or complete reversal of this self or selfishness into Truth that constitutes Transmutation. The enlightened man has abandoned the delusion that the evil in others has power to hurt and subdue him, and he has grasped the profound truth that he is only overthrown by the evil in himself. He therefore ceases to blame others for his sins and sufferings, and applies himself to purifying his own heart. In this reversal of his mental attitude, he transmutes the lower selfish forces into the higher moral attributes. The base ore of error is cast into the fire of sacrifice, and there comes forth the pure gold of Truth.

Such a man stands firm and unmoved when assailed by outward things. He is self's master, not its slave. He has ceased to identify himself with the impulses of passion, and has identified himself with Truth. He has overcome evil, and has become merged in Good. He knows both error and Truth, and has abandoned error and brought himself into harmony with Truth. He returns good for evil. The more he is assailed by evil from without, the greater is his opportunity of manifesting the good from within. That which supremely differentiates the fool from the wise man is this—that the fool meets passion with passion, hatred with hatred, and returns evil for evil; whereas the wise man meets passion with peace, hatred with love, and returns good for evil.

Evil Is The Denial of Good

Men inflict suffering upon themselves through the active instrumentality of their own unpurified nature. They rise into perfect peace in the measure that they purify their hearts. The mental energy which men waste in pursuing dark passions is all-sufficient to enable them to reach the highest wisdom when it is turned in the right direction.

As water, when transmuted into steam, becomes

The Wisdom of James Allen III ~

a new, more definite and wide-reaching power, so passion, when transmuted into intellectual and moral force, becomes a new life, a new power for the accomplishment of high and unfailing purposes.

Mental forces, like molecular, have their opposite poles or modes of action. Where the negative pole is, there also is the positive. Where ignorance is, wisdom is possible. Where passion abounds, peace awaits. Where there is much suffering, much bliss is near. Sorrow is the negation of joy; sin is the opposite of purity; evil is the denial of good. Where there is an opposite, there is that which is opposed. The adverse evil, in its denial of the good, testifies to its presence. The one thing needful, therefore, is the turning around from the negative to the positive; the conversion of the heart from impure desires to pure aspirations; the transmutation of passional forces into moral powers.

The wise purify their thoughts. They turn from bad deeds and do good deeds. They put error behind them and approach Truth. Thus do they rise above the allurements of sin, above the torments of temptation, above the dark world of sorrow, and enter the Divine Consciousness, the Transcendent Life.

Transcendence

WHEN A MAN PASSES from the dark stage of temptation to the more enlightened stage of transmutation, he has become a saint. A saint is one who perceives the need for self-purification, who understands the way of self-purification, and who has entered that way and is engaged in perfecting himself.

But there comes a time in the process of transmutation when, with the decrease of evil and the accumulation of good, there dawns in the mind a new vision, a new consciousness, a new man. When this is reached, the saint has become a sage; he has passed from the human life to the divine life. He is "born again," and there begins for him a new round of experiences. He wields a new power; a new universe opens out before his spiritual gaze. This is the stage of transcendence. This I call the Transcendent Life.

When there is no more consciousness of sin; when anxiety and doubt, and grief and sorrow, are ended; when lust and animosity, and anger and envy, no more possess the thoughts; when there remains in the mind no vestige of blame towards others for one's own condition, and when all conditions are seen to be good because they are the result of causes, so that no event can afflict the mind, then Transcendence is attained. Then the limited personality is outgrown, and the divine life is known; evil is transcended, and Good is all-in-all.

The Transcendent Life Is Ruled by Principles

The divine consciousness is not an intensification of the human; it is a new form of consciousness. It springs from the old, but it is not a continuance of it. Born of the lower life of sin and sorrow, after a period of painful torment, it yet transcends that life and has no part in it, just as the perfect flower transcends the seed from which it sprang.

As passion is the keynote of the self-life, so serenity is the keynote of the transcendent life. Rising into it, man is lifted above disharmony and disturbance. When Perfect Good is realized and known, not as an opinion or an idea, but as an experience or a possession, then calm vision is acquired, and tranquil joy abides through all hardships.

The Transcendent Life is ruled, not by passions, but by principles. It is founded not upon fleeting impulses, but upon abiding laws. In its clear atmosphere the orderly sequence of all things is revealed, so that there is seen to be no room for sorrow, anxiety, or regret.

While men are involved in the passions of self, they burden themselves with cares, and trouble themselves over many things. Above all else, they trouble over their own little, burdened, pain-stricken personality, being anxious for its fleeting pleasures, for its protection and preservation, and for its eternal safety and continuance. Now in the life that is wise and good all this is transcended. Personal interests are replaced by universal purposes, and all cares, troubles, and anxieties concerning the pleasure and the fate of the personality are dispelled like the feverish dreams of a night.

Transcendence Is Beyond Selfishness

Passion is blind and ignorant. It sees and knows only its own gratification. Self recognizes no law; its object is to get and to enjoy. The getting is a graduated scale varying from sensual greed, through many subtle vanities, up to the desire for a personal heaven or personal immortality, but it is self still. It is the old sensual craving coming out in a more subtle and deceptive form. It is longing for some personal delight, along with its accompanying fear that delight should be lost forever.

In the transcendent state, desire and dread are ended, and the thirst for gain and the fear of loss are things that are no more. For where the universal order is seen, and where perennial joy in that good is a normal condition, what is there left to desire? What remains to be feared?

He who has brought his entire nature into conformity and harmony with the law of righteousness, who has made his thoughts pure and his deeds blameless, has entered liberty. He has transcended darkness and mortality, and has passed into light and immortality. For the transcendent state is at first a higher order of morality, then a new form of perception, and at last a comprehensive understanding of the universal moral causation. And this morality, this vision, and this understanding constitute the new consciousness, the divine life.

The transcendent man is he who is above and

~ From Passion to Peace

beyond the dominion of self. He has transcended evil and lives in the practice and knowledge of good. He is like a man who, having long looked upon the world with darkened eyes, is now restored to sight, and sees things as they are.

The Experiences of Good

Evil is an experience, and not a power. If it were an independent power in the universe, it could not be transcended by any being. But though not real as a power, it is real as a condition and an experience, for all experience is of the nature of reality. It is a state of ignorance, of undevelopment and as such it recedes and disappears before the light of knowledge, as the intellectual ignorance of a child vanishes before the gradually accumulating learning, or as darkness dissolves before the rising light.

The painful experiences of evil pass away as the new experiences of good enter into and possess the field of consciousness. And what are the new experiences of good? They are many and beautiful—such as the joyful knowledge of the freedom from sin. They are the absence of remorse and deliverance from all torments of temptation. They are ineffable joy in conditions and circumstances which formerly caused deep affliction, and imperviousness to be hurt by the actions of others. They are great patience and sweetness of character; serenity of mind under all circumstances; and emancipation from doubt, fear, and anxiety. They are freedom from all dislike, envy, and animosity, with the power to feel and act kindly towards those who see fit to constitute themselves as one's enemies or opponents. They are the divine power to give blessings for curses, and to return good for evil; a deep knowledge of the human heart, with a perception of its fundamental goodness; and insight into the law of moral causation and the mental evolution of beings, with a prophetic foresight of the sublime good that awaits humanity. Above all, they are a glad rejoicing in the limitation and impotency of evil, and in the eternal supremacy and power of good.

All these, and the calm, strong, far-reaching life that these imply and contain, are the rich experiences of the transcendent man, along with all the new and varied resources, the vast powers, the quickened abilities, and enlarged capacities that spring to life in the new consciousness.

Evil Must Be Forsaken

Transcendence is surpassing virtue. Evil and good

cannot dwell together. Evil must be abandoned, left behind and transcended before good is grasped and known. When good is practiced and fully comprehended, then all the afflictions of the mind are at an end. For that which is accompanied with pain and sorrow in the consciousness of evil is not so accompanied in the consciousness of good.

Whatsoever happens to the good man cannot cause him perplexity or sorrow, for he knows its cause and issue, knows the good which it is ordained to accomplish in himself, and so his mind remains happy and serene. Though the body of the good man may be bound, his mind is free. Though it be wounded and in pain, joy and peace abide within his heart.

Life Is a School

A spiritual teacher had a pupil who was apt and earnest. After several years of learning and practice, the pupil one day offered a question for discussion which his master could not answer. After days of deep meditation, the master said to his pupil, "I cannot answer the question which you have asked. Have you any solution to offer?" Whereupon the pupil formulated a reply to the question which he had propounded. The master then said to him: "You have answered that which I could not, and henceforth neither I nor any man can instruct you, for now you are indeed instructed by truth. You have soared, like the kingly eagle, where no man can follow. Your work is now to instruct others. You are no longer the pupil, you have become the master."

In looking back on the self-life which he has transcended, the divinely enlightened man sees all the afflictions of that life as though his schoolmasters were teaching and leading him upward. And in the measure that he penetrated their meaning and lifted himself above them, they departed from him. Their mission to teach him having ended, they left him the triumphant master of the field. For the lower cannot teach the higher; ignorance cannot instruct wisdom; evil cannot enlighten good; nor can the pupil set lessons for the master. That which is transcended cannot reach up to that which transcends. Evil can only teach in its own sphere, where it is regarded as master. In the sphere of good it has no place and no authority.

Eventually All Will Achieve Transcendence

The strong traveler on the highway of truth knows no such thing as resignation to evil; he knows only obedience to good. He who submits to evil, saying, "Sin cannot be overcome, and evil must be borne," thereby acknowledges that evil is his master. It is not his master to instruct him, but to bind and oppress him. The lover of good cannot also be a lover of evil, nor can he, for one moment, admit its ascendancy. He elevates and glorifies good, not evil. He loves light, not darkness.

When a man makes truth his master, he abandons error. As he transcends error, he becomes more like his master, until at last he becomes one with truth, teaching it, as a master, by his actions, and reflecting it in his life.

Transcendence is not an abnormal condition; it belongs to the orderly process of evolution. Though, as yet, few have reached it, all will come into it in the course of the ages. And he who ascends into it sins no more, sorrows no more, and is no more troubled. Good are his thoughts, good are his actions, and the good is the tranquil tenor of his way. He has conquered self, and has submitted to truth. He has mastered evil, and has comprehended good. Henceforth neither men nor books can instruct him, for he is instructed by the Supreme Good, the spirit of truth.

Beatitude

WHEN DIVINE GOOD is practiced, life is bliss. Bliss is the normal condition of the good man. Those outer assaults, harassments, and persecutions which bring such sufferings to others, only serve to heighten his happiness, for they cause the deep fountain of good within him to well up in greater abundance.

To have transcendent virtue is to enjoy transcendent happiness. The beatific blessedness which Jesus holds out is promised to those having the heavenly virtues—to the merciful, the pure in heart, the peacemakers, and so on. The higher virtue does not merely and only lead to happiness; it is happiness. It is impossible for a man of transcendent virtue to be unhappy. The cause of unhappiness must be sought and found in the self-loving elements, and not in the self-sacrificing qualities. A man may have virtue, and be unhappy, but not so if he has divine virtue.

Divine Virtue Transcends Human Virtue

Human virtue is mingled with self, and therefore with sorrow. But from divine virtue every taint of self has been purged away, and with it every vestige of misery. One comparison will suffice to illustrate this: a man may have the courage of a lion in attack and self-defense (such courage being a human virtue), but he will not thereby be rendered supremely happy.

However, he whose courage is that of the divine kind which enables him to transcend both attack and defense, and to remain mild, serene, and lovable under attack, such a man will thereby be rendered supremely happy. Moreover, his assailant will be rendered more happy, in that a more powerful good will overcome and cast out the fierce and unhappy evil of the other.

The acquisition of human virtue is a great step towards truth. But the divine way transcends it—truth lies upward and beyond.

Doing good in order to gain a personal heaven or personal immortality is human virtue, but it is not unmixed with self, and not emancipated from sorrow. In the transcendent virtues all is good, and good is all, and there is no personal or ulterior aim. Human virtue is imperfect; it is mixed with the baser, selfish elements, and needs to be transmuted. Divine virtue is unblemished and pure; it is complete and perfect in itself.

The Ten Divine Transcendent Virtues

And what are the transcendent virtues that embody all happiness and joy? They are:

Impartiality; the seeing so deeply into the human heart, and into human actions, that it becomes impossible to take sides with one man or one party against the other, and therefore the power to be perfectly just.

Unlimited Kindness towards all men, women, and all creatures, whether enemies or friends.

Perfect Patience at all times, in all circumstances, and under the severest trials.

Profound Humility; the total surrender of self; the judging of one's own actions as though they were the actions of another.

Stainless Purity of mind and deed. Freedom from all evil thoughts and impure imaginings.

Unbroken Calmness of mind, even in the midst of outward strife, or surrounded by the turmoil of many hardships and difficulties.

Abiding Goodness of heart; impervious to evil; returning good for evil.

Compassion; deep pity for all creatures and beings in their sufferings. Shielding the weak and helpless; and protecting, out of pity, even one's enemies from injury and slander.

Abounding Love toward all living things; rejoicing with the happy and successful, and sympathizing with the sorrowing and defeated.

Perfect Peace toward all things. Being at peace with all the world. A profound reconciliation to the Divine Order of the universe.

The Ten-Jeweled Crown of The Sage

Such are the virtues that transcend both vice and virtue. They include all that virtue embodies, while going beyond it into divine truth. They are the fruits of innumerable efforts to achieve; the glorious gifts of him that overcomes. They constitute the ten-jeweled crown prepared for the calm brow of him who has conquered himself. With these majestic virtues is the mind of the sage adorned. By them he is eternally shielded from sin and sorrow, from harm and hurt, from trouble and turmoil. In them he abides in happiness, a blessedness, a bliss, so pure and tranquil, so deep and high, so far transcending all the fleeting excitements of self, as to be unknown and incomprehensible to the self-seeking consciousness.

The sage has conquered passion and has come to lasting peace. As the mighty mountain remains unmoved by the turbulent ocean that beats at its base, so the mind of the sage, towering in lofty virtue, remains unshaken by the tempests of passion which beat unceasingly upon the shores of life. Good and wise, he is evermore happy and serene. Transcendently virtuous, he lives in beatific bliss.

Peace

WHERE PASSION IS, peace is not; where peace is, passion is not. To know this is to master the first letter in the divine language of perfect deeds. To know that passion and peace cannot dwell together is to be well prepared to renounce the lesser and embrace the greater.

Men pray for peace, yet cling to passion. They foster strife, yet pray for heavenly rest. This is ignorance, profound spiritual ignorance. It is not to know the first letter in the alphabet of things divine.

Hatred and love, strife and peace, cannot dwell together in the same heart. Where one is admitted as a welcome guest, the other will be turned away as an unwelcome stranger. He who despises another will be despised by others. He who opposes his fellow man will himself be resisted. He should not be surprised, and mourn, that men are divided. He should know that he is propagating strife. He should understand his lack of peace.

By Self-Conquest Is Peace Assured

He is brave who conquers another; but he who conquers himself is supremely noble. He who is victorious over another may, in turn, be defeated; but he who overcomes himself will never be subdued.

By the way of self-conquest is Perfect Peace achieved. Man cannot understand it, cannot approach it, until he sees the supreme necessity of turning away from the fierce fighting of things without, and entering the noble warfare against evils within. He who has realized that the enemy of the world is within, and not without; that his own ungoverned thoughts are the source of confusion and strife; that his own unchastened desires are the violators of his peace, and of the peace of the world; such a man is already on the Saintly Way.

If a man has conquered lust and anger, hatred and pride, selfishness and greed, he has conquered the world. He has slain the enemies of peace, and peace remains with him.

Peace does not fight; is not partisan; has no blatant voice. The triumph of peace is an unassailable silence.

He who is overcome by force is not thereby overcome in his heart; he may be a greater enemy than before. But he who is overcome by the spirit of peace is thereby changed at heart. He that was an enemy has become a friend. Force and strife work upon the passions and fears, but love and peace reach and reform the heart.

Peace Shields The Righteous

The pure-hearted and wise have peace in their hearts. It enters into their actions; they apply it in their lives. It is more powerful than strife; it conquers where force would fail. Its wings shield the righteous. Under its protection, the harmless are not harmed. It affords a secure shelter from the heat of selfish struggle. It is a refuge for the defeated, a tent for the lost, and a temple for the pure.

Where peace is practiced, and possessed, and known, then sin and remorse, grasping and disappointment, craving and temptation, desiring and grieving—all the turbulence and torment of the mind—are left behind in the dark sphere of the self to which they belong, and beyond which they cannot go.

Beyond where these dark shadows move, the radiant Plains of Divine Beatitude bask in Eternal Light, and to these, the traveler on the High and Holy Way comes in due time. From the blinding swamps of passion, through the thorny forests of many vanities, across the arid deserts of doubt and despair, he travels on, not turning back nor straying his course. He ever moves toward his sublime destination, until at last he comes, a humble and lowly, yet strong and radiant conqueror, to the beautiful City of Peace.

BOOK FOUR

The Heavenly Life

THE HEAVENLY LIFE
TABLE OF CONTENTS

The Divine Center..297

The Eternal Now..305

The "Original Simplicity"......................................311

The Unfailing Wisdom..317

The Might of Meekness..324

The Righteous Man..332

Perfect Love..335

Perfect Freedom...341

Greatness, Simplicity, and Goodness....................345

Heaven in The Heart..353

The Divine Center

THE SECRET OF LIFE, of abundant life, with its strength, its joy, and its unbroken peace is to find the Divine Center within oneself. It is to live in and from that, instead of in that outer circumference of disturbances—the clamors, cravings, and argumentations which make up the animal and intellectual man. These selfish elements constitute the mere husks of life, and must be thrown away by him who would penetrate to the Central Heart of things—to Life itself.

To not know that within you which is changeless, and defiant of time and death, is not to know anything, but is to play vainly with unsubstantial reflections in the mirror of time. To not find within yourself those passionless Principles which are unmoved by the strifes, shows, and vanities of the world, is to find nothing but illusions which vanish as they are grasped.

He who resolves that he will not rest satisfied with appearances, shadows, and illusions shall, by the piercing light of that resolve, disperse every fleeting fantasy, and will enter into the substance and reality of life. He will learn how to live, and he will live. He will be no slave of passion, no servant of opinion, no enthusiast of fond error. By finding the Divine Center within his own heart, he will be calm, strong, and wise. He will ceaselessly radiate the Heavenly Life in which he lives—which is himself.

Having taken himself to the Divine Refuge within, and remaining there, a man is free from sin. All his yesterdays are as the tide-washed and untrodden sands. No sin shall rise up against him to torment and accuse him and destroy his sacred peace. The fires of remorse shall no longer scorch him, nor can the storms of regret devastate his dwelling-place.

His tomorrows are as seeds which germinate, bursting into the beauty and potency of life. No doubt shall shake his trust, no uncertainty shall rob him of repose. The Present is his, and only in the immortal Present does he live. And it is as the eternal vault of blue above, which looks down silently and calmly, yet radiant with purity and light, upon the upturned and tear-stained faces of the centuries.

The Death of The Ego-Personality

Men love their desires, for gratification seems sweet to them, but its end is pain and emptiness. They love the argumentations of the intellect, for egotism seems most desirable to them, but the fruits thereof are humiliation and sorrow. When the soul has reached the end of gratification and reaped the bitter fruits of egotism, it is ready to receive the Divine Wisdom and to enter into the Divine Life. Only the crucified can be transfigured. Only by the death of self can the Lord of the heart rise again into the immortal life, and stand radiant upon the Mount of Wisdom.

Do you have trials? Every outward trial is the replica of an inward imperfection. You shall grow wise by knowing this, and thereby transmute your trials into active joy. You shall find the Kingdom where trial cannot come. *When wilt thou learn thy lessons, O child of earth!* All your sorrows cry out against you. Every pain is your just accuser, and your griefs are but the shadows of your unworthy and perishable self. The Kingdom of Heaven is yours. How long will you reject it, preferring the lurid atmosphere of Hell—the hell of your own self-seeking self?

Where self or ego is not—there is the Garden of the Heavenly Life and—

> *"There spring the healing streams*
> *Quenching all thirst! there bloom*
>   *the immortal flowers*
> *Carpeting all the way with joy! there throng*
> *Swiftest and sweetest hours!"*

The redeemed sons and daughters of God, those who are glorified in body and spirit, are "bought with a price," and that price is the crucifixion of the personality, the death of the ego-self. Having put away that within which is the source of all discord, they have found the universal music, the abiding joy.

The Choice Is Always Yours

Life is more than motion, it is music. It is more than rest, it is peace. More than work, it is duty. More than labor, it is love. More than enjoyment, it is blessedness. More than money, position, and reputation, it is knowledge, purpose, and strong and high resolve.

Let the impure turn to purity, and they shall be

~ The Heavenly Life

pure. Let the weak resort to strength, and they shall be strong. Let the ignorant fly to knowledge, and they shall be wise. All things belong to man, and he chooses that which he will have. Today he chooses in ignorance, tomorrow he shall choose in wisdom. He shall "work out his own salvation" whether he believes it or not, for he cannot escape himself, nor transfer to another the eternal responsibility of his own soul. By no theological deception shall he trick the law of his being, which shall shatter all his selfish makeshifts and excuses for right thinking and right doing. Nor shall God do for him that which it is destined for his soul to accomplish for itself.

What would you say of a person who, wanting to possess a mansion in which to dwell peacefully, prepared the site and then knelt down and asked God to build the house for him? Would you not say such a man was foolish? And of another man who, having purchased land, set the architects, builders, and carpenters at work to erect the edifice, would you not say that he was wise?

As it is in the building of a material house, so it is in the building of a spiritual mansion. Brick by brick, pure thought upon pure thought, good deed upon good deed, must the habitation of a blameless life rise from its sure foundation until at last it stands out in all the majesty of its faultless proportions. Not by caprice, nor gift, nor favor does a man obtain spiritual realities, but by diligence, watchfulness, energy, and effort.

> *"Strong is the soul, and wise and beautiful*
> *The seeds of God-like power are in us still;*
> *Gods are we, bards, saints, heroes, if we will."*

Building The Inner Mansion

The spiritual heart of man is the Heart of the universe, and, finding that Heart, man finds the strength to accomplish all things. He finds there also the wisdom to see things as they are. He finds there the peace that is divine. At the center of man's being is the music which orders the stars—the Eternal Harmony. He who would find blessedness, let him find himself. Let him abandon every discordant desire, every inharmonious thought, every unlovely habit and deed, and he will find that grace, beauty, and harmony which form the indestructible essence of his own being.

Men fly from creed to creed, and find—unrest. They travel in many lands, and discover—disappointment. They build themselves beautiful mansions, plant pleasant gardens, and reap—boredom and discomfort. Not until a man falls back upon the Truth within himself does he find rest and satisfaction. Not until he builds the inward mansion of faultless conduct does he find endless and incorruptible Joy. Having obtained that, he will infuse it into all his outward doings and possessions.

If a man would have peace, let him exercise the spirit of Peace. If he would find love, let him dwell in the spirit of Love. If he would escape suffering, let him cease to inflict it. If he would do noble things for humanity, let him cease to do cruel things to himself. If he will but quarry the mine of his own soul, he shall find there all the materials for building whatsoever he will, and he shall find there also the central Rock on which to build in safety.

Howsoever a man works to right the world, it will never be righted until he has put himself right. This may be written upon the heart as a mathematical axiom. It is not enough to preach purity, men must cease from lust. To exhort to love, they must abandon hatred. To glorify self-sacrifice, they must yield up self. To adorn with mere words the Perfect Life, they must be perfect.

When a man can no longer carry the weight of his

many sins, let him fly to the Christ, whose throne is the center of his own heart, and he shall become light-hearted, entering the glad company of the Immortals.

When he can no longer bear the burden of his accumulated learning, a man should leave his books, his science, his philosophy, and come back to himself. There, he shall find within, that which he outwardly sought and found not—his own divinity.

He who has found God within ceases to argue about God. Relying upon that calm strength which is not the strength of self, he lives God, manifesting in his daily life the Highest Goodness, which is Eternal Life.

The Eternal Now

NOW IS THE REALITY in which time is contained. It is more and greater than time; it is an ever-present reality. It knows neither past nor future, and is eternally potent and substantial. Every minute, every day, every year is a dream as soon as it has passed, and exists only as an imperfect, and unsubstantial picture in the memory, if it is not entirely obliterated.

Past and future are dreams; now is a reality. All things are now. All power, all possibility, all action is now. Not to act and accomplish now is not to act and accomplish at all. To live in thoughts of what you might have done, or in the dreams of what you mean to do, this is folly. But to put away regret, to anchor anticipation, to do and to work now, this is wisdom.

When a man is dwelling upon the past or future

he is missing the present. He is forgetting to live now. All things are possible now, and only now. Without wisdom to guide him, and mistaking the unreal for the real, a man says, "If I had done so and so last week, last month, or last year, it would have been better with me today." Or, "I know what is best to be done, and I will do it tomorrow."

The selfish cannot comprehend the vast importance and value of the present, and fail to see it as the substantial reality of which past and future are the empty reflections. It may truly be said that past and future do not exist except as negative shadows, and to live in them, that is, in the regretful and selfish contemplation of them—is to miss the reality in life.

"The Present, the Present is all thou hast,
For thy sure possessing;
Like the patriarch's angel, hold it fast,
Till it gives its blessing.

"All which is real now remaineth,
And fadeth never:
The hand which upholds it now sustaineth
The soul forever.

*"Then of what is to be, and of what is to be done,
Why queriest thou?
The past and the time to be are one,
And both are NOW!"*

Now Is The Ideal Time

Man has all power now; but not knowing this, he says, "I will be perfect next year, or in so many years, or in so many lives." The dwellers in the Kingdom of God, who live only in the now, say, "I am perfect now," and refraining from all sin now, and ceaselessly guarding the portals of the mind, not looking to the past nor to the future, nor turning to the left or right, they remain eternally holy and blessed. "Now is the accepted time; now is the day of salvation."

Say to yourself, "I will live in my Ideal now. I will manifest my Ideal now. I will be in my Ideal now. I will not listen to all that tempts me away from my Ideal. I will listen only to the voice of my Ideal." Thus resolving and thus doing, you shall not depart from the Highest, and shall eternally manifest the True.

*"Afoot and lighthearted, I take to the open road.
Henceforth I ask not good fortune: I myself am good fortune.*

*Henceforth I whimper no more, postpone no more,
   need nothing.*
*Done with indoor complaints, libraries, querulous
   criticisms.*
Strong and content, I take to the open road."

Cease to tread every byway of dependence, every winding side-way that tempts your soul into the shadow-land of the past and the future, and manifest your native and divine strength now. Come out into "the open road."

Tomorrow Is Too Late for Anything

That which you would be, and hope to be, you may be now. Non-accomplishment resides in your perpetual postponement, and having the power to postpone, you also have the power to accomplish—to perpetually accomplish. Realize this truth, and you shall be today, and every day, the ideal man of whom you dreamed.

Virtue consists in fighting sin day after day, but holiness consists in leaving sin, unnoticed and ignored, to die by the wayside. And this is done, can only be done, in the living now. Say not to your soul, "You shall be purer tomorrow;" but rather say, "You shall be pure now." Tomorrow is too late for anything, and he who sees his help and salvation in tomorrow shall continuously fail and fall today.

Did you fall yesterday? Did you sin grievously? Having realized this, leave it instantly and forever, and watch that you do not sin now. While you are bewailing the past, every gate of your soul remains unguarded against the entrance of sin now. You shall not rise by grieving over the irremediable past, but by remedying the present.

The foolish man, loving the boggy sidepath of procrastination rather than the firm Highway of Present Effort, says, "I will rise early tomorrow. I will get out of debt tomorrow. I will carry out my intentions tomorrow." But the wise man, realizing the momentous import of the Eternal Now, rises early today; keeps out of debt today; carries out his intentions today; and so never departs from strength, peace, and ripe accomplishment.

That which is done now remains; that which is done tomorrow does not appear. It is wisdom to leave that which has not arrived, and to attend to that which is; and to attend to it with such a consecration of soul and concentration of effort as shall leave no possible loophole for regret to creep in.

Throw Off Your Illusions

When a man's spiritual comprehension is clouded by the illusions of self, he says, "I was born on such a day, so many years ago, and shall die at my allotted time." But he was not born, neither will he die, for how can that which is immortal, which eternally is, be subject to birth and death? Let a man throw off his illusions, and then he will see that the birth and death of the body are the mere incidents of a journey, and not a beginning and end.

Looking back to happy beginnings, and forward to mournful endings, a man's eyes are blinded, so that he beholds not his own immortality. His ears are closed, so that he hears not the ever-present harmonies of Joy. And his heart is hardened, so that it pulsates not to the rhythmic sounds of Peace.

The universe, with all that it contains, is now. Put out your hand, O seeker, and receive the fruits of Wisdom! Cease your greedy striving, your selfish sorrowing, your foolish regretting, and be content to live. Act now, and, lo! all things are done. Live now, and, behold! you are in the midst of plenty. Be now, and know that you are perfect.

The "Original Simplicity"

LIFE IS SIMPLE. Being is simple. The universe is simple. Complexity arises in ignorance and self-delusion. The "Original Simplicity" of Lao-Tze is a term expressive of the universe as it is, and not as it appears. Looking through the woven network of his own illusions, man sees interminable complication and unfathomable mystery, and so loses himself in the labyrinths of his own making.

Let a man put away egotism, and he will see the universe in all the beauty of pristine simplicity. Let him annihilate the delusion of the personal "I," and he will destroy all the delusions which spring from that "I." He will thus "re-become a little child," and will "revert to Original Simplicity."

When a person succeeds in entirely forgetting (annihilating) his personal self, he becomes a mirror in which the universal Reality is faultlessly reflected. He is awakened, and henceforth he lives, not in dreams, but realities.

The Universe Is One Perfect Whole

Pythagoras saw the universe in the ten numbers. But even this simplicity may be further reduced, and the universe ultimately can be found to be contained in the number ONE, for all the numerals and their infinite complications are but additions of the One.

Let life cease to be lived as a fragmentary thing, and let it be lived as a perfect Whole. The simplicity of the Perfect will then be revealed. How shall the fragment comprehend the Whole? Yet how simple that the Whole should comprehend the fragment. How shall sin perceive Holiness? Yet how plain that Holiness should understand sin.

He who would become the Greater let him abandon the lesser. In no form is the circle contained, but in the circle all forms are contained. In no color is the radiant light imprisoned, but in the radiant light all colors are embodied. Let a man destroy all the forms of self, and he shall understand the Circle of Perfection. Let him submerge, in the silent depths of his being, the varying colors of his thoughts and desires, and he shall be illuminated with the White Light of Divine Knowledge.

In the perfect chord of music the single note, though forgotten, is indispensably contained, and the drop of water becomes of supreme usefulness by losing itself in the ocean. Sink yourself compassionately in the heart of humanity, and you shall reproduce the harmonies of Heaven. Lose yourself in unlimited love toward all, and you shall create enduring works and shall become one with the eternal Ocean of Bliss.

The Road Back to "Original Simplicity"

Man evolves outward to the periphery of complexity, and then involves backward to the Central Simplicity. When a man discovers that it is mathematically impossible for him to know the universe before knowing himself, he then starts upon the Way which leads to the Original Simplicity. He begins to unfold from within, and as he unfolds himself, he unfolds the universe.

Cease to speculate about God, and find the all-embracing Good within you, then you shall see the emptiness and vanity of speculation, knowing yourself one with God.

He who will not give up his secret lust, his covetousness, his anger, his opinion about this or that, can see or know nothing. He will remain a dullard in the school of Wisdom, though he be learned in the colleges.

If a man would find the Key of Knowledge, let him find himself. Your sins are not you; they are not any part of yourself. They are diseases which you have come to love. Cease to cling to them, and they will no longer cling to you. Let them fall away, and you shall stand revealed. You shall then know yourself as Comprehensive Vision, Invincible Principle, Immortal Life, and Eternal Good.

The Simplicity of "Original Simplicity"

The impure man believes impurity to be his rightful condition, but the pure man knows himself as pure being. He also, penetrating the Veils, sees all others as pure being. Purity is extremely simple and needs no argument to support it. Impurity is interminably complex, and is ever involved in defensive argument. Truth lives itself. A blameless life is the only witness of Truth. Men cannot see, and will not accept the witness until they find it within themselves. Having found it, a man becomes silent while surrounded by his fellows. Truth is so simple that it cannot be found in the region of argument and advertisement, and so silent that it is only manifested in actions.

~ The Heavenly Life

So extremely simple is Original Simplicity, that a man must let go his hold of everything before he can perceive it. The great arch is strong by virtue of the hollowness underneath, and a wise man becomes strong and invincible by emptying himself.

Humility, Patience, Love, Compassion, and Wisdom—these are the dominant qualities of Original Simplicity; therefore the imperfect cannot understand it. Wisdom only can understand Wisdom. Therefore the fool says, "No man is wise." The imperfect man says, "No man can be perfect," and he therefore remains where he is—foolish and imperfect.

Though he may live with a perfect man all his life, he shall not behold his perfection. Humility he will call cowardice. Patience, love, and compassion he will see as weakness. Wisdom will appear to him as folly. Faultless discrimination belongs to the Perfect Whole, and resides not in any part. Therefore men are exhorted to refrain from judgement until they have themselves manifested the Perfect Life.

All Problems Vanish in "Original Simplicity"

Arriving at Original Simplicity, haziness disappears, and the universal transparency becomes apparent. He who has found the indwelling Reality of his own being has found the original and universal Reality. Knowing the Divine Heart within, all hearts are known, and the thoughts of all people become his who has become master of his own thoughts. The good man, therefore, does not defend himself, but molds the minds of others to his own likeness.

As the problematical transcends crudity, so Pure Goodness transcends the problematical. All problems vanish when Pure Goodness is reached; therefore, the good man is called "The slayer of illusions." What problem can vex one where sin is not? O you who strive so loudly and rest not—retire into the holy silence of your own being, and live therefrom. Finding Pure Goodness you shall tear in two the veil of the Temple of Illusion, and you shall enter into the Patience, Peace, and transcendent Glory of the Perfect. For Pure Goodness and Original Simplicity are one.

The Unfailing Wisdom

A MAN SHOULD BE SUPERIOR to his possessions, his body, his circumstances and surroundings, and the opinions of others and their attitude towards him. Until he is this, he is not strong and steadfast. He should also rise superior to his own desires and opinions; and until he is this, he is not wise.

The man who identifies himself with his possessions will feel that all is lost when these are lost. He who regards himself as the outcome and the tool of circumstances will weakly fluctuate with every change in his outward condition; and great will be the unrest and pain of he who seeks to stand upon the praise of others.

To detach oneself from every outward thing, and to rest securely upon the inward virtue, this is the Unfailing Wisdom. Having this Wisdom, a man will be the same whether in riches or poverty. Wealth cannot add to his strength, nor can impoverishment rob him of his serenity. Neither can riches defile him who has washed away all his inward defilement, nor can the lack of them degrade him who has ceased to degrade the temple of his soul.

Everything Happens for The Best

To refuse to be enslaved by any outward thing or happening, and to regard all things and happenings as for your use, and for your education, this is Wisdom. To the wise all occurrences are good, and, having no eye for evil, they grow wiser every day. They utilize all things, and thus put all things under their feet. They see all their mistakes as soon as they are made, and accept them as lessons of intrinsic value, knowing that there are no mistakes in the Divine Order. They thus rapidly approach the Divine Perfection. They are moved by none, yet learn from all. They crave love from none, yet give love to all.

To learn, and not to be shaken; to love where one is not loved; herein lies the strength which shall never fail a man. The man who says in his heart, "I will teach all men, and learn from none," will neither teach nor learn while in that frame of mind, but will remain in his folly.

You Must Be Willing to Learn

All strength and wisdom, power and knowledge a

man will find within himself, but he will not find it in egotism. He will only find it in obedience, submission, and the willingness to learn. He must obey the Higher, and not glorify himself in the lower. He who stands upon egotism, rejecting reproof, instruction, and the lessons of experience, will surely fall. Yea, he has already fallen.

A great teacher once said to his disciples, "Those who shall be a lamp unto themselves, rely upon themselves only, and do not rely upon any external help. They hold fast to the Truth as their lamp, and seek their salvation in the Truth alone. They shall not look for assistance to any besides themselves. It is they among my disciples who shall reach the very topmost height! But they must be willing to learn."

The wise man is always anxious to learn, but never anxious to teach, for he knows that the true teacher is in the heart of every man, and must ultimately be found there by all. The foolish man, being governed largely by vanity, is very anxious to teach, but unwilling to learn, not having found the Holy Teacher within who speaks wisdom to the humbly listening soul. Be self-reliant, but let your self-reliance be saintly and not selfish.

Folly and wisdom, weakness and strength are within a man, and not in any external thing, neither do they spring from any external cause. A man cannot be strong for another, he can only be strong for himself. He cannot overcome for another, he can only overcome of himself.

You may learn from another, but you must accomplish for yourself. Put away all external props, and rely upon the Truth within you. A creed will not bear a man up in the hour of temptation. He must possess the inward knowledge which slays temptation. A speculative philosophy will prove a shadowy thing in the time of calamity. A man must have the inward Wisdom which puts an end to grief.

What You Seek Is Already Within You

Goodness, which is the aim of all religions, is distinct from religions themselves. Wisdom, which is the aim of every philosophy, is distinct from all philosophies. The Unfailing Wisdom is found only by constant practice in pure thinking and well-doing; by harmonizing one's mind and heart to those things which are beautiful, lovable, and true.

In whatever condition a man finds himself, he can always find the True; and he can find it only by so utilizing his present condition as to become strong and wise. The hankering after rewards, and the cowardly

~ The Heavenly Life

fear of punishment, let them be put away forever. Rather, let a man joyfully bend to the faithful performance of all his duties, forgetting himself and his worthless pleasures, and live strong, pure, and self-contained. So shall he surely find the Unfailing Wisdom, the Godlike patience and strength.

> *"The situation that has not its Duty, its Ideal, was never yet occupied by man...*
> *Here or nowhere is thy Ideal.*
> *Work it out therefrom, and, working, believe, live, be free.*
> *The Ideal is in thyself, the impediment, too, is in thyself;*
> *Thy condition is but the stuff thou art to shape that same Ideal out of.*
> *What matters whether such stuff be of this sort or that, so the form thou give it be heroic, be poetic?*
> *Oh, thou that pinest in the imprisonment of the Actual, and criest bitterly to the gods for a kingdom wherein to rule and create, know this of a truth:*
> *The thing thou seekest is already within thee, here and now, couldest thou only see!"*

All that is beautiful and blessed is in yourself, not in your neighbor's wealth. Are you poor? You are poor indeed if you are not stronger than your poverty! Have you suffered calamities? Well, will you cure your calamity by adding anxiety to it? Can you mend a broken vase by weeping over it, or restore a lost delight by your lamentations? There is no evil that will not vanish if you will but wisely meet it. The Godlike soul does not grieve over that which has been, is, or will be, but perpetually finds the Divine Good, and gains wisdom by every occurrence.

The Supreme Law of Life Is Love

Fear is the shadow of selfishness, and cannot live where loving Wisdom is. Doubt, anxiety, and worry are unsubstantial shades in the underworld of self, and shall no more trouble him who will climb the serene altitudes of his soul. Grief, also, will be forever dispelled by him who will comprehend the Law of his being.

He who so comprehends shall find the Supreme Law of Life, and he shall find that it is Love, that it is imperishable Love. He shall become one with that Love, and loving all, with his mind freed from all hatred and folly, he shall receive the invincible protection which Love affords. Claiming nothing, he shall

~ The Heavenly Life

suffer no loss. Seeking no pleasure, he shall find no grief. And employing all his powers as instruments of service, he shall evermore live in the highest state of blessedness and bliss.

Know this—you make and unmake yourself. You stand and fall by what you are. You are a slave if you prefer to be; you are a master if you will make yourself one. Build upon your animal and intellectual opinions, and you build upon the sand. Build upon virtue and holiness, and no wind nor tide shall shake your strong abode. So shall the Unfailing Wisdom uphold you in every emergency, and the Everlasting Arms gather you to your peace.

> "*Lay up each year*
> *Thy harvest of well-doing, wealth that kings*
> *Nor thieves can take away. When all the things*
> *Thou callest thine, goods, pleasures, honors fall,*
> *Thou in thy virtue shall survive them all.*"

The Might of Meekness

THE MOUNTAIN BENDS NOT to the fiercest storm, but it shields the fledgling and the lamb. And though all men tread upon it, regardless, it provides them with protection and bears them up upon its deathless bosom. So it is with the meek or humble man. Shaken and disturbed by none, he compassionately bends to shield the lowliest creature. And though he may be despised, he lifts all men up, and lovingly protects them.

As glorious as the mountain in its silent might is the divine man in his silent Humility. Like its form, his loving comparison is expansive and sublime. Truly his body, like the mountain's base, is fixed in the valleys and the mists; but the summit of his being is eternally bathed in cloudless glory, and lives with the Silences.

He who has found Meekness or Humility has found divinity. He has realized the divine consciousness and knows himself as divine. He also knows all others as divine, though they know it not themselves, being asleep and dreaming. Humility is a divine quality, and as such is all powerful. The meek man overcomes by not resisting, and by allowing himself to be defeated, he attains the Supreme Conquest.

The man who conquers another by force is strong; but he who conquers himself with Meekness is mighty. He who conquers another by force will himself likewise be conquered. He who conquers himself by Gentleness will never be overthrown, for the human cannot overcome the divine. The gentle man is triumphant in defeat.

Socrates lives the more by being put to death. In the crucified Jesus the risen Christ is revealed. And Stephen in receiving his stoning defies the hurting power of stones.

The Attributes of Humility

That which is real cannot be destroyed, but only that which is unreal. When a man finds that within him which is real, which is constant, abiding, changeless, and eternal, he enters into that Reality and becomes gentle. All the powers of darkness will come against him, but they will do him no harm, and will at last depart from him.

The humble man is found in the time of trial.

When other men fall, he stands. His patience is not destroyed by the foolish passions of others. When they come against him, he does not "strive nor cry." He knows the utter powerlessness of all evil, having overcome it in himself, and lives in the changeless strength and power of divine Good.

Humility is one aspect of the operation of that changeless Love which is at the heart of all things, and is therefore an imperishable quality. He who lives in it is without fear, knowing the Highest, and having the lowest under his feet.

The gentle man shines in the darkness, and flourishes in obscurity. Humility cannot boast, nor advertise itself, nor thrive on popularity. It is practiced, and is seen or not seen. Being a spiritual quality it is perceived only by the eye of the spirit. Those who are not spiritually awakened see it not, nor do they love it, being enamored of, and blinded by, worldly shows and appearances.

Nor does history take note of the humble man. The glory of history is that of strife and self-aggrandizement; the meek man's is the glory of peace and gentleness. History chronicles the earthly, not the heavenly acts. Yet though he lives in obscurity, the man of humility cannot be hidden. (How can light be hid?) He continues to shine even after he has with-

~ The Heavenly Life

drawn himself from the world, and he is worshiped by the world which knew him not.

Humility Resists None and Conquers All

That the gentle man should be neglected, abused, or misunderstood is reckoned by him as of no account, and therefore not to be considered, much less resisted. He knows that all such weapons are the flimsiest and most ineffectual of shadows. To them, therefore, who give him evil, he gives good in return. He resists none, and thereby conquers all.

He who imagines that he can be injured by others, and who seeks to justify and defend himself against them, does not understand Meekness or Humility. He does not comprehend the essence and meaning of life.

> *"He abused me, he beat me, he defeated me, he robbed me.—*
> *In those who harbor such thoughts hatred will never cease...*
> *For hatred ceases not by hatred at any time;*
> *Hatred ceases by love."*

What, you say your neighbor has spoken falsely about you? Well, what of it? Can a falsity hurt the true

The Wisdom of James Allen III ~

you? That which is false is false, and that is the end of it. Falseness is without life, and without power to hurt any except him who seeks to be hurt by it. It is nothing to you that your neighbor should speak falsely of you, but it is much to you that you seek to resist him and justify yourself, for, by so doing, you give life and vitality to your neighbor's false claim. And by so doing, you are injured and distressed in return. Take all evil out of your own heart, then shall you see the folly of resisting it in another.

You say you'll be trodden upon? You are trodden on already if you think you are. The injury that you see as coming from another comes only from yourself. The wrong thought, or word, or act of another has no power to hurt you unless you galvanize it into life by your passionate resistance, and so receive it into yourself.

If any man slanders me, that is his concern, not mine. I have to deal with my own soul, not with my neighbors. Though all the world may misjudge me, it is no business of mine. But that I should possess my soul in Purity and Love, that is all my business. There shall be no end to strife until men cease to justify themselves.

He who would have wars cease let him cease to defend any party—let him cease to defend even himself. Not by strife can peace come, but by ceasing from strife. The glory of Caesar resides in the resistance of his enemies. They resist and fall. Give to Caesar that which Caesar demands, and Caesar's glory and power are gone. Thus by submission does the meek man conquer the strong man. But it is not that outward show of submission which is slavery, it is that inward and spiritual submission which is freedom.

Humility Is Non-Resistance in Thought

Claiming no rights, the gentle man is not troubled with self-defense and self-justification. He lives in love, and therefore comes under the immediate and vital protection of the Great Love which is the Eternal Law of the universe. He neither claims nor seeks his own. Thus do all things come to him, and all the universe shields and protects him.

He who says, "I have tried Humility, and it has failed," has not tried Humility. It cannot be tried as an experiment. It is only arrived at by unreserved self-sacrifice. Humility or meekness does not consist merely in non-resistance in action; it consists preeminently in non-resistance in thought. It is ceasing to hold or to have any selfish, condemnatory, or retaliatory thoughts. The meek man, therefore, cannot "take offense" or have his "feelings hurt," living above hatred, folly, and vanity. Gentleness can never fail.

O you who search for the Heavenly Life! Strive after Gentleness and Humility. Increase your patience and forbearance day by day. Bid your tongue to cease from all harsh words. Withdraw your mind from selfish arguments, and refuse to brood upon your wrongs. By so living, you shall carefully tend and cultivate the pure and delicate flower of Humility in your heart, until at last, its divine sweetness, purity, and beauteous perfection shall be revealed to you, and you shall become gentle, joyful, and strong.

Humility Lifts The Veils of Illusion

Complain not that you are surrounded by irritable and selfish people. Rather, rejoice that you are so favored as to have your own imperfections revealed to you, and that you are so placed as to necessitate within you a constant struggle for self-mastery and the attainment of perfection. The more there is of harshness and selfishness around you, the greater the need of your gentleness, humility, and love. If others seek to wrong you, all the more it is needful that you should cease from all wrong, and live in love. If others preach meekness, humility, and love, and do not practice these, trouble not, nor be annoyed. Rather, in the silence of your heart, and in your contact with others, practice these things, and they shall preach themselves. And though you utter no declamatory word, and stand before no gathered audience, you shall teach the whole world.

As you become meek and humble, you shall learn the deepest secrets of the universe. Nothing is hidden from him who overcomes himself. Into the cause of causes you shall penetrate, and lifting, one after another, every veil of illusion, you shall reach at last the inmost Heart of Being. Thus becoming one with Life, you shall know all life, and, seeing into causes, and knowing realities, you shall no longer be anxious about yourself, and others, and the world. You shall see that all things are engines of the Great Law. Canopied with gentleness, you shall bless where others curse; love where others hate; forgive where others condemn; yield where others strive; give up where others grasp; lose where others gain. And in their strength they shall be weak; and in your weakness you shall be strong. Yea, you shall mightily prevail. He that has not unbroken gentleness, has not Truth:

> *"Therefore when Heaven would save a man,*
> *it enfolds him with gentleness."*

The Righteous Man

THE RIGHTEOUS MAN is invincible. No enemy can possibly overcome or confound him; and he needs no other protection than that of his own integrity and holiness.

As it is impossible for evil to overcome Good, so the righteous person can never be brought low by the unrighteous. Slander, envy, hatred, malice—these can never reach him, nor cause him any suffering—and those who try to injure him only succeed ultimately in bringing disgrace upon themselves.

The righteous man, having nothing to hide, committing no acts which require stealth, and harboring no thoughts and desires which he would not like others to know, is fearless and unashamed. His step is firm, his body upright, and his speech direct and without ambiguity. He looks everyone in the face. How can he who wrongs none reflect fear? How can he who

~ The Heavenly Life

deceives none feel ashamed? And ceasing from all wrong he can never be wronged; ceasing from all deceit he never can be deceived.

The righteous man, performing all his duties with scrupulous diligence, and living above sin, is invulnerable at every point. He who has slain the inward enemies of virtue can never be brought low by any outward enemy; neither does he seek protection against them, righteousness being an all-sufficient protection.

The Unrighteous Man

The unrighteous man is vulnerable at almost every point. Living in his passions, the slave of prejudices, impulses, and ill-formed opinions, he is continually suffering (as he imagines) at the hands of others. The slanders, attacks, and accusations of others cause him great suffering because they have a basis of truth in himself. Not having the protection of righteousness, he endeavors to justify and protect himself by resorting to retaliation and fallacious argument, and even to deception and deceit.

The partially righteous man is vulnerable at all those points where he falls short of righteousness. Should the righteous man fall from his righteousness, and give way to one sin, his invincibility is gone, for he has thereby placed himself where attack and accusation can justly reach and injure him, because he has first injured himself.

If a man suffers or is injured through the instrumentality of others, let him look to himself. Let him put aside self-pity and self-defense, and he will find in his own heart the source of all his woe.

Suffering Cannot Reach The Righteous

No evil can happen to the righteous man who has cut off the source of evil in himself. Living in the All-Good, and abstaining from error in thought, word, and deed, whatever happens to him is good. Neither can any person, event, or circumstance cause him suffering, for the tyranny of circumstance is utterly destroyed for him who has broken the bonds of sin.

The suffering, the sorrowing, the weary, and broken-hearted ever seek a sorrowless refuge, a haven of perpetual peace. Let such men fly to the refuge of the righteous life. Let them come now and enter the haven of the sinless state, for sorrow cannot overtake the righteous. Suffering cannot reach him who does not waste in self-seeking his spiritual substance; and he cannot be afflicted by weariness and unrest whose heart is at peace with all.

Perfect Love

THE CHILDREN OF LIGHT, who abide in the Kingdom of Heaven, see the universe, and all that it contains, as the manifestation of one Law—The Law of Love. They see Love as the molding, sustaining, protecting, and perfecting Power immanent in all things animate and inanimate. To them Love is not merely and only a rule of life, it is the Law of Life, it is Life itself. Knowing this, they order their whole life in accordance with Love, not regarding their own personality. By thus practicing obedience to the Highest, to divine Love, they become conscious partakers of the power of Love, and so arrive at perfect Freedom as Masters of Destiny.

The universe is preserved because Love is at the heart of it. Love is the only preservative power. Whenever there is hatred in the heart of man, he imagines the Law to be cruel, but when his heart is mellowed by Compassion and Love, he perceives that the Law is Infinite Kindness. So kind is the Law that it protects man against his own ignorance. Man, in his puny efforts to subvert the Law by attaching undue importance to his own little personality, brings upon himself such trains of suffering that he is at last compelled, in the depth of his afflictions, to seek for Wisdom. Finding Wisdom, he finds Love, and knows it as the Law of his being, the Law of the universe.

Love does not punish. Man punishes himself by his own hatred, by striving to preserve evil which has no life by which to preserve itself, and by trying to subvert Love, which can neither be overcome nor destroyed, being of the substance of Life. When a man burns himself, does he accuse the fire? Therefore, when a man suffers, let him look for some ignorance or disobedience within himself.

Love Eliminates Suffering

Love is Perfect Harmony, pure Bliss, and therefore contains no element of suffering. Let a man think no thought and do no act which is not in accordance with pure Love, and suffering shall trouble him no more. If a man would know Love, and partake of its

~ The Heavenly Life

undying bliss, he must practice it in his heart. He must become Love.

He who always acts in the spirit of Love is never deserted, is never left in a dilemma or difficulty, for Love (impersonal Love) is both Knowledge and Power. He who has learned how to Love has learned how to master every difficulty, how to transmute every failure into success, how to clothe every event and condition in garments of blessedness and beauty.

The way to Love is by self-mastery, and, traveling that way, a man builds himself up in Knowledge as he proceeds. Arriving at Love, he enters into full possession of body and mind, by right of the divine Power which he has earned.

"Perfect Love casteth out fear." To know Love is to know there is no harmful power in the whole universe. Even sin itself, which the worldly and unbelieving imagine is so unconquerable, is known as a very weak and perishable thing, that shrinks away and disappears before the compelling power of Good. Perfect Love is perfect Harmlessness. He who has destroyed, in himself, all thoughts of harm, and all desire to harm, receives universal protection, and knows himself to be invincible.

Perfect Love is perfect Patience. Anger and irritability cannot dwell with it nor come near it. It sweetens every bitter occasion with the perfume of holiness, and transmutes trial into divine strength. Complaint is foreign to it. He who loves bewails nothing, but accepts all things and conditions as heavenly guests. He is therefore constantly blessed, and sorrow does not overtake him.

Other Attributes of Perfect Love

Perfect Love is perfect Trust. He who has destroyed the desire to grasp can never be troubled with the fear of loss. Loss and gain alike are foreign to him. When he steadfastly maintains a loving attitude toward all, and pursues, in the performance of his duties, a constant and loving activity, Love protects him and evermore supplies him in fullest measure with all that he needs.

Perfect Love is perfect Power. The wisely loving heart commands without exercising any authority. All things and all men obey him who obeys the Highest. He thinks, and lo! he has already accomplished. He speaks, behold! a world hangs upon his every word! He has harmonized his thoughts with the Imperishable and Unconquerable Forces, and for him, weakness and uncertainty are no more. His every thought is a pur-

~ The Heavenly Life

pose; his every act an accomplishment. He moves with the Great Law, not setting his puny personal will against it. Thus, he becomes a channel through which the Divine Power can flow in unimpeded and beneficent expression. He has thus become Power itself.

Perfect Love is perfect Wisdom. The man who loves all is the man who knows all. Having thoroughly learned the lessons of his own heart, he knows the tasks and trials of other hearts, and adapts himself to them gently and without ostentation. Love illuminates the intellect. Without it the intellect is blind, cold, and lifeless. Love succeeds where the intellect fails; sees where the intellect is blind; knows where the intellect is ignorant. Reason is only completed in Love, and is ultimately absorbed in it. Love is the Supreme Reality in the universe, and as such it contains all Truth.

Infinite tenderness enfolds and cherishes the universe; therefore the wise man is gentle, childlike, and tender-hearted. He sees that the one thing which all creatures need is Love, which he gives generously and freely. He knows that all occasions require the adjusting power of Love, and he ceases from harshness.

To the eye of Love all things are revealed, not as an infinity of complex effects, but in the light of Eternal Principles, out of which spring all causes and effects, and back into which they return. "God is Love;" therefore there is nothing more perfect than Love. He who would find pure Knowledge let him find pure Love.

Perfect Love is perfect Peace. He who dwells with it has completed his pilgrimage in the underworld of sorrow. With mind calm and heart at rest, he has banished the shadows of grief, and knows the deathless Life.

If you would perfect yourself in Knowledge, perfect yourself in Love. If you would reach the Highest, ceaselessly cultivate a loving and compassionate heart.

Perfect Freedom

THERE IS NO BONDAGE in the Heavenly Life. There is Perfect Freedom. This is its great glory. This Supreme Freedom is gained only by obedience. He who obeys the Highest cooperates with the Highest, and so masters every force within himself and every condition without.

A man may choose the lower and neglect the Higher, but the Higher is never overcome by the lower: herein lies the revelation of Freedom. Let a man choose the Higher and abandon the lower; he shall then establish himself as an Overcomer, and shall realize Perfect Freedom.

To give the reins to inclination is the only slavery; to conquer oneself is the only freedom. The slave to self loves his chains, and will not have them broken for fear he would be depriving himself of some cherished delight. He clings to gratifications and vanities, regarding freedom from them as an empty and undesirable condition. He thus defeats and enslaves himself.

By self-enlightenment is Perfect Freedom found. While a man remains ignorant of himself, of his desires, of his emotions and thoughts, and of the inward causes which mold his life and destiny, he has neither control nor understanding of himself. He will remain in bondage to passion, sorrow, suffering, and fluctuating fortune. The Land of Perfect Freedom lies through the Gate of Knowledge.

Inner Freedom Brings Outward Freedom

All outward oppression is but the shadow and effect of the real opposition within. For ages the oppressed have cried for liberty, and a thousand man-made laws have failed to give it to them. They can give freedom only to themselves. They shall find it only in obedience to the Divine Laws which are inscribed upon their hearts. Let them resort to the inward Freedom, and the shadow of oppression shall no more darken the earth. Let men cease to oppress themselves and no man shall oppress his brother.

Men legislate for an outward freedom, yet continue to render such freedom impossible of achievement by fostering an inward condition of enslavement. They thus pursue a shadow without, and ignore the substance within. Man will be free when he is freed from self. All outward forms of bondage and oppression will cease to be when man ceases to be the willing bond-slave of passion, error, and ignorance. Freedom is to the free.

While men cling to weakness they cannot have strength. While they love darkness they can receive no light. So long as they prefer bondage they can enjoy no liberty. Strength, light, and freedom are ready now, and can be had by all who love them, who aspire to them. Freedom does not reside in cooperative aggression, for this will always produce, reactively, cooperative defense—warfare, hatred, party strife, and the destruction of liberty. Freedom resides in individual self-conquest. The emancipation of humanity is frustrated and withheld by the self-enslavement of the unit. You who cry out to man and God for liberty, liberate yourself!

Freedom Does Not Shirk From Duty

The Heavenly Freedom is freedom from passion, from cravings, from opinions, from the tyranny of the flesh, and the tyranny of the intellect—this first, and then all outward freedom, as effect to cause. The

Freedom that begins within, and extends outwardly until it embraces the whole man, is an emancipation so complete, all-embracing, and perfect as to leave no galling fetter unbroken. Free your soul from all sin, and you shall walk a freed and fearless man in the midst of a world of fearful slaves. Seeing you, many slaves shall take heart and shall join you in your glorious freedom.

He who says, "My worldly duties are irksome to me; I will leave them and go into solitude, where I shall be as free as the air," and thinks to gain freedom thus, will only find a harder slavery. The tree of Freedom is rooted in Duty. He who would pluck its sweet fruits must discover joy in Duty.

Glad-hearted, calm, and ready for all tasks is he who is freed from self. Irksomeness and weariness cannot enter his heart, and his divine strength lightens every burden so that its weight is not felt. He does not run away from Duty with his chains about him, but breaks them and stands free.

Make yourself pure. Make yourself proof against weakness, temptation, and sin. For only in your own heart and mind shall you find that Perfect Freedom for which the whole world sighs and seeks in vain.

Greatness, Simplicity, and Goodness

GOODNESS, SIMPLICITY, GREATNESS—these three are one and this trinity of perfection cannot be separated. All greatness springs from goodness, and all goodness is profoundly simple. Without goodness there is no greatness. Some men pass through the world as destructive forces, like the tornado or the avalanche, but they are not great. They are to greatness as the avalanche is to the mountain. The work of greatness is enduring and preservative, and not violent and destructive. The greatest souls are the most gentle.

Greatness is never obtrusive. It works in silence, seeking no recognition. This is why it is not easily perceived and recognized. Like the mountain it towers up in its vastness, so that those in its immediate vicinity, who receive its shelter and shade, do not see it. Its sublime grandeur is only beheld as they recede from it. The great man is not seen by his contemporaries. The majesty of his form is only outlined by its recession in time. This is the awe and enchantment of distance.

Most men occupy themselves with the small things; their houses, trees, and lands. Few contemplate the mountain at whose base they live, and fewer still attempt to explore it. But in the distance these small things disappear, and then the solitary beauty of the mountain is perceived. Popularity, noisy obtrusiveness, and shallow show, these superficialities rapidly disappear, and leave behind no enduring mark; whereas greatness slowly emerges from obscurity, and endures forever.

All Genius Is Impersonal Truth

Jewish Rabbi and rabble alike saw not the divine beauty of Jesus; they saw only an unlettered carpenter. To his acquaintances, Homer was only a blind beggar, but the centuries reveal him as Homer the immortal poet. Two hundred years after the farmer of Stratford (and all that is known of him) has disappeared, the real Shakespeare is discerned. All true

~ The Heavenly Life

genius is impersonal. It belongs not to the man through whom it is manifested; it belongs to all. It is a diffusion of pure Truth; the Light of Heaven descending on all mankind.

Every work of genius, in whatever department of art, is a symbolic manifestation of impersonal Truth. It is universal, and finds a response in every heart in every age and race. Anything short of this is not genius, is not greatness. That work which defends a religion perishes; it is religion that lives. Theories about immortality fade away; immortal man endures. Commentaries upon Truth come to the dust; Truth alone remains. That only is true in art which represents the True; that only is great in life which is universally and eternally true. The True is the Good; and the Good is the True.

Every immortal work springs from the Eternal Goodness in the human heart, and it is clothed with the sweet and unaffected simplicity of goodness. The greatest art is, like nature, artless. It knows no trick, no pose, no studied effort. There are no stage tricks in Shakespeare. He is the greatest of dramatists because he is the simplest. The critics, not understanding the wise simplicity of greatness, always condemn the loftiest work. They cannot discriminate between the childish and the childlike. The True, the Beautiful, the Great, is always childlike, and is perennially fresh and young.

Greatness Is Good and Always Simple

The great man is always the good man; he is always simple. He draws from, nay, lives in, the inexhaustible fountain of divine Goodness within. He inhabits the Heavenly Places; communes with the vanished great ones; lives with the Invisible. He is inspired, and breathes the airs of Heaven.

He who would be great, let him learn to be good. He will therefore become great by not seeking greatness. Aiming at greatness a man arrives at nothingness; aiming at nothingness he arrives at greatness. The desire to be great is an indication of littleness, of personal vanity and obtrusiveness. The willingness to disappear from the public eye, the utter absence of self-aggrandizement is the witness of greatness.

Littleness seeks and loves authority. Greatness is never authoritative, and it thereby becomes the authority to which future generations appeal. He who seeks, loses. He who is willing to lose, wins all men. Be your simple self, your better self, your impersonal self, and lo! you are great! He who selfishly seeks authority shall succeed only in becoming a trembling

~ The Heavenly Life

apologist courting protection behind the back of acknowledged greatness. He who will become the servant of all humanity, desiring no personal authority, shall live simply, and shall be called great.

> *"Abide in the simple and noble regions of thy life, obey thy heart, and thou shalt reproduce the foreworld again."*

Forget your own little self, and fall back upon the Universal self, and you shall reproduce, in living and enduring forms, a thousand beautiful experiences. You shall find within yourself that simple goodness which is greatness.

Cast Away Your Petty Ego

"It is as easy to be great as to be small," says Emerson; and he utters a profound truth. Forgetfulness of self is the whole of greatness, as it is the whole of goodness and happiness. In a fleeting moment of self-forgetfulness the smallest soul becomes great. Extend that moment indefinitely, and there is a great soul, a great life. Cast away your personality (your petty cravings, vanities, and ambitions) as a worthless garment, and dwell in the loving, compassionate, selfless regions of your soul, and you are no longer small—you are great.

Claiming personal authority, a man descends into littleness; practicing goodness, a man ascends into greatness. The presumptuousness of the small may, for a time, obscure the humility of the great, but it is at last swallowed up by it, as the noisy river is lost in the calm ocean.

The vulgarity of ignorance and the pride of learning must disappear. Their worthlessness is equal. They have no part in the Soul of Goodness. If you would do, you must be. You shall not mistake information for Knowledge; you must know yourself as pure Knowledge. You shall not confuse learning with Wisdom; you must apprehend yourself as undefiled Wisdom.

What Do You Want to Do?

Would you write a living book? You must first live; you must draw around you the mystic garment of a manifold experience, and must learn, in enjoyment and suffering, gladness and sorrow, conquest and defeat, that which no book and no teacher can teach you. You must learn of life, of your soul. You must tread the Lonely Road, and must become; you must be. Then, write your book, and it shall live; it shall be

~ The Heavenly Life

more than a book. Let your book first live in you, then will you live in your book.

Would you carve a statue that shall captivate the ages, or paint a picture that shall endure? You must acquaint yourself with the divine Beauty within you. You must comprehend and adore the Invisible Beauty. You must know the principles which are the soul of Form. You must perceive the matchless symmetry and faultless proportions of Life, of Being, of the Universe. Thus knowing the eternally True, you will carve or paint the indescribably beautiful.

Would you produce an imperishable poem? You must first live your poem. You must think and act rhythmically. You must find the never-failing source of inspiration in the loving places of your heart. Then shall immortal lines flow from you without effort. As the flowers in the wood and field spontaneously spring, so shall beautiful thoughts grow in your heart and, enshrined in words as molds to their beauty, shall subdue the hearts of humanity.

Would you compose such music as shall gladden and uplift the world? You must adjust your soul to the Heavenly Harmonies. You must know that yourself, that life and the universe is music. You must touch the chords of Life. You must know that Music is everywhere; that it is the Heart of Being. Then will you hear with your spiritual ear the Immortal Symphonies.

Would you preach the living word? You must forego yourself, and become that Word. You must know one thing—that the human heart is good, is divine. You must live one thing—Love. You must love all, seeing no evil, thinking no evil, believing no evil. Then, though you speak but little, your every act shall be a power, your every word, a precept. By your pure thought, your selfless deed, though it appears hidden, you will preach, down the ages, to untold multitudes of aspiring souls.

To him who chooses Goodness, sacrificing all, is given that which is more than and includes all. He becomes the possessor of the Best, communes with the Highest, and enters the company of the Great.

The greatness that is flawless, rounded, and complete is above and beyond all art. It is Perfect Goodness in manifestation. Therefore, the greatest souls are always teachers.

Heaven in The Heart

THE TOIL OF LIFE CEASES when the heart is pure. When the mind is harmonized with the Divine Law the wheel of drudgery ceases to turn, and all work is transmuted into joyful activity. The pure hearted are the lilies of the field, which toil not, yet are fed and clothed from the abundant storehouse of the All-Good. But the lily is not lethargic. It is ceaselessly active, drawing nourishment from earth, air, and sun. By the Divine Power immanent within it, it builds itself up, cell by cell, opening itself to the light, growing and expanding towards the perfect flower.

So it is with those who, having yielded up self-will, have learned to cooperate with the Divine Will. They grow in grace, goodness and beauty, freed from anxiety, and without friction and toil. They never work in vain; there is no wasted action. Every thought, act, and thing done is subservient to the Divine Purpose, and adds to the sum-total of the world's happiness.

Heaven is in the heart. They will look for it in vain who look elsewhere. In no outward place will the soul find Heaven until it finds it within itself. For wherever the soul goes, its thoughts and desires will go with it. However beautiful may be the outward dwelling-place, if there is sin within, there will be darkness and gloom without, for sin always casts a dark shadow over the pathway of the soul—the shadow of sorrow.

Heaven Is Here and Everywhere

This world is beautiful, transcendently and wonderfully beautiful. Its beauties and inspiring wonders cannot be numbered; yet, to the sin-sodden mind, it appears as a dark and joyless place. Where passion and self are, there is hell, and there are all the pains of hell. Where Holiness and Love are, there is Heaven, and there are all the joys of Heaven.

Heaven is here. It is also everywhere. It is wherever there is a pure heart. The whole universe is abounding with joy, but the sin-bound heart can neither see, hear, nor partake of it. No one is, or can be, arbitrarily shut out from Heaven; each shuts himself out. Its Golden Gates are eternally ajar, but the selfish cannot find them. They mourn, yet see not; they cry, but hear not. Only to those who turn their eyes to

~ The Heavenly Life

heavenly things; their ears to heavenly sounds, are the happy Portals of the Kingdom revealed, and they enter and are glad.

All life is gladness when the heart is right, when it is attuned to the sweet chords of holy Love. Life is Religion, Religion is Life, and all is joy and gladness. The jarring notes of creeds and politics, the black shadows of sin, let them pass away forever. They cannot enter the Door of Life; they form no part of Religion. Joy, Music, Beauty—these belong to the true order of things. They are the texture of the universe; of these is the divine garment of life woven. Pure Religion is glad, not gloomy. It is light without darkness or shadow.

Despondency, disappointment, grief—these are the reflex aspects of pleasurable excitement, self-seeking, and desire. Give up the latter, and the former will forever disappear; then there remains the perfect Bliss of Heaven.

Heaven Is Your Home

Abounding and unalloyed Happiness is a man's true life. Perfect Blessedness is his rightful portion. When he loses his false life and finds the true he enters into full possession of his Kingdom. The

Kingdom of Heaven is man's Home; and it is here and now; it is in his own heart, and he is not left without Guides, if he wills to find it. All man's sorrows and sufferings are the result of his own self-elected estrangement from the Divine Source, the All-Good, the Father, the Heart of Love. Let him return to his Home. His peace awaits him.

The Heavenly-hearted are without sorrow and suffering because they are without sin. What the worldly-minded call troubles they regard as pleasant tasks of Love and Wisdom. Troubles belong to hell; they do not enter Heaven.

This is so simple it should not appear strange. If you have a trouble it is in your own mind, and nowhere else. You make it, it is not made for you. It is not in your task; it is not in that outward thing. You are its creator, and it derives its life from you only. Look upon all your difficulties as lessons to be learned, as aids to spiritual growth, and lo! they are difficulties no longer! This is one of the pathways up to Heaven.

The Magic of Love

To transmute everything into Happiness and Joy, this is supremely the work and the duty of the Heavenly-minded man. To reduce everything to wretchedness and deprivation is the process which the worldly-minded unconsciously pursue. To live in Love is to work in Joy. Love is the magic that transforms all things into power and beauty. It brings plenty out of poverty, power out of weakness, loveliness out of deformity, sweetness out of bitterness, light out of darkness, and produces all blissful conditions out of its own substantial but indefinable essence.

He who loves can never want. The universe belongs to Goodness, and it therefore belongs to the good man. It can be possessed by all without limitation or shrinking, for Goodness and the abundance of Goodness (material, mental and spiritual abundance), is inexhaustible. Think lovingly, speak lovingly, act lovingly, and your every need shall be supplied. You shall not walk in desert places, and no danger shall overtake you.

Love sees with faultless vision, judges true judgement, acts in wisdom. Look through the eyes of Love, and you shall see everywhere the Beautiful and True. Judge with the mind of Love, and you shall err not, shall wake no wail of sorrow. Act in the spirit of Love, and you shall strike undying harmonies upon the Harp of Life.

Make no compromise with self. Cease not to strive until your whole being is swallowed up in Love.

To love all and always—this is the Heaven of heavens.

> *"Let there be nothing within thee that is not very*
> *beautiful and very gentle, and then there will be*
> *nothing without thee*
> *that is not beautified and softened*
> *by the spell of thy presence."*

All that you do, let it be done in calm wisdom. Do not from desire, impulse, or opinion; this is the Heavenly way of action.

Purify your thought-world until no stain is left, and you will ascend into Heaven while living in the body. You will then see the things of the outward world clothed in all beautiful forms. Having found the Divine Beauty within ourselves, it springs to life in every outward thing. To the beautified soul the world is beautiful.

Hell Is Preparation for Heaven

Undeveloped souls are merely unopened flowers. The perfect Beauty lies concealed within, and will one day reveal itself to the full-orbed light of Heaven. Seeing men thus, we stand where evil is not, and where the eye beholds only good. Herein lies the

~ The Heavenly Life

peace, patience, and beauty of Love—it sees no evil. He who loves thus becomes the protector of all men. Though in their ignorance they may hate him, he shields and loves them.

What gardener is so foolish as to condemn flowers because they do not develop in a day? Learn to love and you shall see in all souls, even those who are "degraded," the Divine Beauty. You shall know that it will not fail to come forth in its own season. This is one of the Heavenly Visions, it is out of this that Gladness comes.

Sin, sorrow, suffering—these are the dark gropings of the unopened soul for Light. Open the petals of your soul and let the glorious Light stream in.

Every sinful soul is an unresolved harmony. It shall at last strike the Perfect Chord, and swell the joyful melodies of Heaven.

Hell is the preparation for Heaven; and out of the debris of its ruined hovels are built pleasant mansions wherein the perfected soul may dwell.

Night is only a fleeting shadow which the world casts, and sorrow is but a transient shade cast by the self. "Come out into the Sunlight." Know this, O reader! that you are divine. You are not cut off from the Divine except in your own unbelief. Rise up, O Son of

God! and shake off the nightmare of sin which binds you. Accept your heritage—the Kingdom of Heaven! Drug your soul no longer with the poison of false beliefs. You are not "a worm of the dust" unless you choose to make yourself one.

Heaven Is Within You

You are a divine, immortal, God-born being, and this you may know if you will seek and find. Cling no more to your impure and groveling thoughts, and you shall know that you are a radiant and celestial spirit, filled with pure and lovable thoughts. Wretchedness, sin, and sorrow are not your lot in life unless you accept them as such. If you do this, they will be your portion hereafter, for these things are not apart from your soul-condition. They will go wherever you go; they are only within you.

Heaven, not hell, is your portion here and always. It only requires you to take that which belongs to you. You are the master, and you choose whom you will serve. You are the maker of your state, and your choice determines your condition. What you pray and ask for (with your mind and heart, not merely with your lips), this you will receive. You are served as you serve. You are conditioned as you condition. You garner in your own.

~ The Heavenly Life

Heaven is yours; you have but to enter in and take possession. Heaven means Supreme Happiness, Perfect Blessedness. It leaves nothing to be desired; nothing to be grieved over. It is complete satisfaction now and in this world. It is within you; and if you do not know this, it is because you persist in turning the back of your soul upon it. Turn round and you shall behold it.

Come and live in the sunshine of your being. Come out of the shadows and the dark places. You are framed for Happiness. You are a child of Heaven. Purity, Wisdom, Love, Abundance, Joy, and Peace—these are the eternal Realities of the Kingdom, and they are yours, but you cannot possess them in sin. They have no part in the Realm of Darkness. They belong to "the Light which lighteth every man that cometh into the world," the Light of spotless Love. They are the heritage of the holy Christ-Child who shall come to birth in your soul when you are ready to divest yourself of all impurities. They are your real Self.

But he whose soul has been safely delivered of the wonderful Joy-Child does not forget the travail of the world.

FIN

More Titles in the James Allen Wisdom Series

The Wisdom of James Allen
5 Classic Works including *As a Man Thinketh*
by James Allen Edited by Andy Zubko
Softcover 384 pp. $10.95 ISBN: 1-889606-00-6

For over a hundred years, James Allen's best-known work, *As a Man Thinketh*, has inspired thousands of readers to live more successful and effective lives. *The Wisdom of James Allen* contains *As a Man Thinketh* with four more of his classic works: *The Path to Prosperity*, *The Mastery of Destiny*, *The Way of Peace*, and *Entering the Kingdom*.

EXCERPT FROM *WISDOM OF JAMES ALLEN*:

The greatest achievement was at first and for a time a dream. The oak sleeps in the acorn; the bird sleeps in the egg; and in the highest vision of the soul a waking angel stirs. Dreams are the seedlings of realities....

Your circumstances may be uncongenial, but they shall not long remain so if you but perceive an Ideal and strive to reach it. You cannot travel within and stand still without....Whatever your present environment may be, you will fall, remain, or rise with your thoughts, your Vision, your Ideal. You will become as small as your controlling desire; as great as your dominant aspiration.   —From *As a Man Thinketh*

More Titles in the James Allen Wisdom Series

The Wisdom of James Allen II
3 Classics from the author of *As a Man Thinketh*
by James Allen Edited by Andy Zubko
Softcover 336 pp. $10.95 ISBN: 1-889606-07-3

Book Two contains three more works from the author of *As a Man Thinketh* that provide insight into understanding and triumphing over our life conditions. Book Two includes these three James Allen titles: *Light on Life's Difficulties*, *Above Life's Turmoil*, and *The Life Triumphant*.

EXCERPT FROM *WISDOM OF JAMES ALLEN II*:

We cannot alter external things, nor shape other people to our liking, nor mold the world to our wishes; but we can alter internal things—our desires, passions, thoughts—we can shape our liking to other people, and we can mold the inner world of our own mind in accordance with wisdom, and so reconcile it to the outer world of men and things. The turmoil of the world we cannot avoid, but the disturbances of the mind we can overcome. The duties and difficulties of life claim our attention, but we can rise above all anxiety concerning them. Surrounded by noise, we can yet have a quiet mind; involved in responsibilities, the heart can be at rest; in the midst of strife, we can know abiding peace.

—**From *Above Life's Turmoil***

More Titles in the James Allen Wisdom Series

The Wisdom of James Allen IV

3 Classics from the author of *As a Man Thinketh*
by James Allen   Edited by Andy Zubko
Softcover 352 pp. $10.95 ISBN: 1-889606-51-0
(Available by Fall 2004)

Book Four combines three more inspirational works from the author of *As a Man Thinketh*, to help readers understand the principles of prosperity and success. Book Four includes: *Foundation Stones to Happiness and Success, Men and Systems*, and *Eight Pillars of Prosperity*.

EXCERPT FROM *WISDOM OF JAMES ALLEN IV*:

Prosperity is at first a spirit, an attitude of mind, a moral power, a life, which manifests outwardly in the form of plenty, happiness, and joy. Just as a man cannot become a genius by writing poems, essays, and plays, but must acquire the soul of genius—when the writing will follow as effect to cause—so one cannot become prosperous by hoarding up money, and gaining property and possessions, but must develop and acquire the soul of virtue—when the material accessories will follow as effect to cause—for the spirit of virtue is the spirit of joy, and it contains within itself all abundance, all satisfaction, and all fullness of life.

—From *The Eight Pillars of Prosperity*

More Titles in the James Allen Wisdom Series

The Wisdom of James Allen V

4 Classics from the author of *As a Man Thinketh*
by James Allen Edited by Andy Zubko
Softcover 352 pp. $10.95 ISBN: 1-889606-11-1
(Available by Summer 2005)

Book Five features four more inspirational works from the author of *As a Man Thinketh*. Book Five includes these four works: *Man: King of Mind, Body, and Circumstance*, *The Shining Gateway*, *Through the Gate of Good*, and *The Divine Companion*.

EXCERPT FROM *WISDOM OF JAMES ALLEN V*:

The kingdom over which man is destined to rule with undisputed sway is that of his own mind and life. This kingdom is not separate from the universe and is not confined to itself alone. It is intimately related to entire humanity, to nature, to the current of events in which it is, for the time being, involved, and to the vast universe. Thus mastery of this kingdom embraces the mastery of the knowledge of life. It lifts a man into the supremacy of wisdom, bestowing upon him the gift of insight into human hearts, giving him the power to distinguish between good and evil...and to know the nature and consequences of deeds.

—From *Man: King of Mind, Body,*

More Titles in the James Allen Wisdom Series

The Wisdom of James Allen VI

2 Classics from the author of *As a Man Thinketh*
by James Allen   Edited by Andy Zubko
Softcover   352 pp. $10.95   ISBN: 1-889606-13-8
(Available by Fall 2005)

Book Six concludes the James Allen Wisdom series with two final inspirational works from the author of *As a Man Thinketh*. Book Six combines: *Morning and Evening Thoughts*, and *Meditations: A Year Book*.

EXCERPT FROM *WISDOM OF JAMES ALLEN VI*:

The way of Love is the Way of Life—Immortal Life—and the beginning of that way consists in getting rid of our carpings, quarrelings, fault-findings, and suspicions. If we are to grow in Love, we must begin at the beginning, and remove from our minds all mean and suspicious thoughts about our fellow-workers and fellow-men. We must learn to treat them with large-hearted freedom, and to perceive the right reasons for their actions, to excuse them on grounds of personal right and personal freedom when their opinions, methods, or actions are contrary to us. Thus shall we come at last to love them with that Love of which St. Paul speaks, a Love that is a permanent principle.

—From *Meditations: A Year Book*

From the Editor of The Wisdom of James Allen

Treasury of Spiritual Wisdom
A Collection of 10,000 Inspirational Quotations
Compiled by Andy Zubko
Softcover 528 pp. $19.95 ISBN: 1-884997-10-4

"*...a compendium of over 10,000 sagely chosen short sayings.*" —**Publishers Weekly**

"*This 'Bartlett's Quotations for the Soul' is a massive collection of inspirational quotations from sources as diverse as Joan Rivers, Jesus, and the Upanishads, covering topics ranging from Abundance and Desire to Self-esteem and Work....appropriate for use by students, teachers, and speakers, this handy reference will be a strong addition to all collections. Recommended.*"
—**Library Journal**

EXCERPTS FROM *TREASURY OF SPIRITUAL WISDOM*:

"*The poor man's charity is to wish the rich man well...*"—**Anonymous** (from "Charity")

"*Never does the human soul appear so strong as when it forgives revenge and dares forgive an injury...*"
—**Edwin H. Chapin** (from "Forgiveness")

"*Man's ultimate aim is the realization of God, and all his activities—social and religious—have to be guided by the ultimate aim of the vision of God...*"
—**Mohandas Gandhi** (from "Self-Realization")